Whiskey Tango Foxtrot

REMEMBRANCES OF MY ... MARINES

Dedication

I dedicate WHISKEY TANGO FOXTROT to all military personnel;
past, present, and future.
Especially those with who I served.
Thank you for your service.
Semper Fidelis

Table of Contents

Acknowledgments

I AM INDEBTED to:

Janice Stevens, my main mentor. The kindest mentor anyone could have. Her encouragement was constant, unwavering;

The Writing for Publication participants, my other mentors, for their observations, encouragement, and friendship;

The counselors and staff at the Fresno Vet Center, especially Ken Hall and Herman Barretto. They guided me to the door of healing. I opened it and passed through.

My children, Tom and Andy, just because.

My wife, Fran, for her devotion, support, and love throughout the years.

Love you all,

Tom

Prologue
Why the Marines

"Navy Brat." That's what I was, a "Navy Brat." That's what you are when your dad is a career Navy man.

Before I completed sixth-grade, Washington, D. C., Hawaii, Guam, and Japan had been home. That was life in the military. San Diego, California was home port. After the sixth-grade, we anchored permanently there.

Ahh, San Diego in the '60s. Terrific time and place. Junior high and high school to boot. It was all the normal things; discover girls, go steady, proms, Friday night football games and dances, theater arts, worry about becoming a father. I played baseball, football, soccer, and ice hockey. And, of course, I surfed. Didn't everybody back then, especially in Southern California?

Every day possible was spent at the beach. Sometimes, I would go at first light to catch the early morning glass. Wade out, lay my surfboard onto the water, climb on, paddle out past the break, push up and through the smooth glassy waves, spin around, pick the largest one of a set, paddle hard, catch it, stand up and jet down its face, turn sharply at the bottom, spraying mist high into the crisp sea air, and fly back up the wave then rocket back down. I might be a little late to my first class. It was worth it. Most times the surf was up.

After high school graduation, on to college.

I wanted to be a fighter pilot in the Marine Corps, which meant I had to get a college degree. A program called Platoon Leaders Class would qualify me to live that dream. I took all the tests, passed them, and was all set to start. The final step to qualify was a physical.

The Marine Corps sent me to Los Angeles for one of those all day physicals. The kind of physical that fine checks everything. All went perfectly until the last exam, the eye exam. That's when I found out I was almost blind. The ophthalmologist asked, "Who are you trying to fool? You're way out in left field." He explained the problem with my eyes and gave me a prescription for eyeglasses. He told me it wasn't my fault. The problem was hereditary. Terrific, my parents had done me in. It was their fault.

Thank you, Mom and Dad.

The Marine Corps advised me I did not qualify for the flight program due to my poor eyesight. I did, however, qualify for the ground program. I turned down that offer. Despondent and depressed did not begin to express how I felt. My life was over.

I continued college. Joined a fraternity. Flunked out.

The Viet Nam War heated up. It wouldn't be long before the draft board would send me greetings. I wanted to join the Marine Corps, not be drafted into the Army. I beat them to the punch by enlisting.

I worked four months in the aerospace industry. A ton of money found its way into my pockets. The blue-collar work didn't tax my brain. I quit and enlisted in the Marine Corps on a delayed entry program. I had three months to kill before going on active duty. With that ton of money, I lived those three months at the beach, out of my '57 Ford two-door station-wagon.

I reported for active duty on August 1, 1966.

I am often asked, "Why did you join the Marine Corps?"

My dad and my mom's dad were career Navy men. I lived my entire life in the Navy. Following in their footsteps did not appeal to me. Through them, I had lived a career in the Navy.

I didn't want to be in the Coast Guard. Too much like the Navy.

I didn't want to be in the Army. Bunch of wimps.

I didn't want to be a part of the Air Force. Ugly blue uniforms. Worse, they wanted four years.

That left the Marines, tough sons of bitches, first to fight, ferocious fighters, mean motor scooters and bad go-getters. Make it in the Marine Corps, you make it anywhere. And, only a three year enlistment, enough time to decide if I wanted to make a career of it.

Plus, Marines wore those great looking Dress Blue uniforms.

Oh, yeah. And, I wanted to fight for my country, keep South Viet Nam from the clutches of the communists.

What else could a know-it-all 18 year old ask for? It all made sense. Perfect logic. Count me in.

Members of my family, each in their own way, supported me. Their first reactions didn't seem so:

Dad, "You would've had a nice, warm place to sleep every night if you had joined the Navy."

Grandma, "Your grandpa's just turned over in his grave! You're going to get killed! I know it!" Thanks, Grandma.

A sense of indestructibility and invincibility was the attitude of us Baby Boomers. We knew we were indestructible. We knew we weren't the one who would die, it would be someone else.

We were invincible. We could not be defeated.

I was invincible. I would not be defeated.

Even so, if it is my time to go, it wouldn't matter if I am in Viet Nam, or in the waters off La Jolla Shores waiting for the next big wave, or on I-5, headed to Disneyland.

1966
Boot Camp

Reporting In

I ENLIST IN the Marine Corps in San Diego, California. After swearing in, they send me to Los Angeles, where I spend the night with a bunch of other recruits in a seedy old downtown hotel.

What do a bunch of teenagers do when on their own, away from home, with meal money issued to them? Be rowdy, whoop it up, get a wino to buy beer for them, and stay up all night, of course.

First thing in morning, I shave off my mustache. I want to be as inconspicuous as possible upon arrival at Marine Corps Recruit Depot, San Diego, California. After breakfast at the hotel's greasy spoon café, day long processing keeps us on the move. Finally, we load onto a bus bound back to San Diego for boot camp. Late at night, we arrive. At last. In no time, I'll be a Marine.

The bus comes to a halt. The door opens. A sharp-looking Marine Sergeant steps into the bus.

"Welcome to the United States Marine Corps Recruit Depot.

"NOW GET THE HELL OFF MY BUS, YOU PIECES OF CRAP, YOU SCUM OF THE EARTH, AND PLANT YOUR STINKIN' FLAT FEET ON THOSE YELLOW FOOTPRINTS! MOVE! MOVE! MOVE, MAGGOTS!"

The Sergeant is the biggest, meanest son of a bitch I ever came across. He is huge. With the loudest booming voice I ever heard. It rattles the bus windows. We rattle the entire bus trampling over each other to get off the bus as fast as we can. Some fall down. Others trip or leap over each other.

"GET UP! GET UP! GET UP, YOU CLUMSY CLOWNS! GET ON THOSE DAMN FOOTPRINTS! NOW! NOW! NOW, NUMBSKULLS!"

We plant our feet on the yellow footprints. Three other Sergeants swarm all about. They are everywhere. Next to us, behind us, in front of us, in our faces, in our ears, all over us. Eyes of crazy men! Snarling at us! All at once! Faces so close I feel their breath, the heat of intense wrath!

"EYES ON THE GOURD IN FRONT OF YOU! DO NOT MOVE YOUR EYES! STAND STRAIGHT! HANDS DOWN THE SIDES OF YOUR LEGS. SHOULDERS BACK! DO NOT MOVE, NOT A MUSCLE, NOT A TWITCH! GUM? DO I SEE SOME OF YOU PUKES CHEWING GUM? SWALLOW IT! SWALLOW IT! SWALLOW IT!"

One of the Sergeants grabs a guy by the hair.

"WHOA, LOOKY HERE. NICE LONG BLONDE HAIR. PRETTY BOY. YOU MUST BE A FAG! ARE YOU SOME SORT OF FUCKING FAG?"

"Ah...."

"SHUT THE HELL UP, YOU SLIMY PIECE OF SHIT! I DID NOT TELL YOU TO SPEAK. YOU WILL NOT SPEAK UNLESS YOU ARE TOLD TO DO SO. EYES STRAIGHT AHEAD! DO NOT MOVE! EYES STRAIGHT AHEAD. DO NOT LOOK AT ME, MAGGOT!"

"I...."

"I? I? I? YOU ARE NOT AN I! YOU ARE A PRIVATE, THE LOWEST THING IN MY MARINE CORPS! THIS IS AN EYE!" He presses his thumb into the guy's eye.

"YOU WILL REFER TO YOURSELF AS PRIVATE! DO YOU UNDERSTAND?"

"Yes, Sir! The Private wishes...."

"WISHES? DO I LOOK LIKE YOUR FUCKIN' FAIRY GODMOTHER?"

"No, Sir."

"....OR SOME GODDAM GENIE?"

"No, Sir. The Private wants...."

"WANTS? THE PRIVATE WANTS? THE MARINE CORPS WILL TELL YOU WHAT YOU WANT! YOU DO NOT WANT ANYTHING UNTIL THE MARINE CORPS TELLS YOU WHAT TO WANT! AND WHEN TO WANT IT! DO YOU UNDERSTAND?"

"Yes, Sir."

"YOU WANT NOTHING! YOU WANT TO SAY NOTHING AND YOU WANT TO SAY NOTHING NOW!"

Suddenly, it is quiet. Still. Nothing moves. No one breathes. The three Sergeants stand in front of us. Somehow, they keep from tearing us to shreds. It's amazing how much I see with peripheral vision. Others look like I feel. Scared shitless.

The Sergeant in between and slightly in front of the other two, growls, "THE ONLY WORDS OUT OF YOUR MUSHY MOUTHS ARE YES, SIR AND NO, SIR. DO YOU UNDERSTAND?"

A weak smattering of, "Yes, Sir."

This ignites a reaction from all three Sergeants.

Sudden steps toward us with an, "ARGH!"

Some of us lean back. A few step off the yellow footprints.

"NOBODY TOLD YOU TO MOVE, YOU SISSIES! STAY ON THOSE FOOTPRINTS! EYES STRAIGHT AHEAD!"

Quiet, still again.

"SON OF A BITCH! A BUNCH OF PUSSIES! NO BALLS AT ALL! AGAIN, THE ONLY WORDS OUT OF YOUR MOUTHS ARE YES, SIR AND NO, SIR. DO YOU UNDERSTAND?"

Scattered, but a little louder, "Yes, Sir?"

"AAARRRRRGGGGGHHHHH! WE CAN'T HEAR YOU! TRY AGAIN!"

"Yes, Sir."

"STILL CAN'T HEAR YOU, GIRLS!"

Louder, but not together, "Yes, Sir."

"SHUT UP! SHUT UP! SHUT UP! CLOSE YOUR SEWER TRAPS! EVERYTHING COMING OUT OF THEM STINKS! BUNCH OF SMELLY, WEAK-ASSES!"

Again, quiet. The Sergeants menacingly stalk around us, through us. None of us dare move, flinch, breathe. They end up in front of us. Again.

The famous haircut. Simple. Everything gone. Nothing left. Not enough to run a wash cloth through.

The first issue of a Marine Corps uniform. A yellow sweatshirt with a big red Marine Corps emblem on the chest, gray sweatpants, white boxer shorts, white tee shirts, white sweat socks, white sneakers, and olive drab hat with the Marine Corps emblem stenciled on the brow.

Uniforms clutched to our chests, the Sergeants herd us into a dimly lit room. Long tables, panels dividing them into individual stations, fill the room.

"GO TO A STATION!"

We stampede to stations. A cardboard box sits inside each station.

"TAKE OFF YOUR LEFT SHOE."

I pull my left foot up, rip off my shoe.

"HOLD IT UP IN YOUR LEFT HAND."

As I do, I see others follow suit.

"PUT IT IN THE BOX."

We do.

"TAKE OFF YOUR RIGHT SHOE.

"HOLD IT UP IN YOUR RIGHT HAND.

"PUT IT IN THE BOX."

So on, until we are naked.

Step by step, as directed. I seal the box, fill out an address label to send the box to Mom. Place the label on the box. When finished, stand there; naked, motionless, staring off to nowhere.

They tell us to dress. Item by item.

"TAKE THE BOXERS IN BOTH HANDS, OPENING TO THE FRONT."

Easy enough.

"BEND DOWN AND STEP INTO THE LEG OPENINGS ONE AT A TIME, LEFT LEG FIRST, THEN THE RIGHT LEG."

Almost toppling over, I pull them on.

And so on, with the final item being the hat.

"TAKE THE COVER. PULL IT DOWN TIGHT OVER YOUR GOURD."

Cover? Must be the hat. That's all that's left.

Looking snazzy in our sharp new uniforms, outside we go. Lined up, four abreast, arms interlocked, as instructed, our rudimentary column moves forward, I hope, for some place to sleep.

No one in sight. Nothing visible. We struggle through the dark.

"Left.

"Right.

"Left.

"Right."

Slowly.

"KEEP YOUR EYES FORWARD! DON'T LOOK AROUND! SHOULDERS BACK! STAND STRAIGHT!

"Left.

"Right.

"Left.

"Right."

Tedious. I don't know whether to laugh or crap my pants. I figure it's best to do neither.

"YOU ARE NOTHING BUT A BUNCH OF SHEEP. AND WE ARE YOUR SHEPHERDS. WE ARE YOUR MOMMIES AND YOUR DADDIES. YOU DO NOTHING UNLESS WE TELL YOU TO. YOUR ASSES ARE OURS.

"WHAT DO SHEEP SAY?"

"Baa?" Softly.

"DON'T STOP. SAY IT! SAY IT! SAY IT!"

"Baa."

"Left."

"Baa."

"Right."

"Baa."

"Left."

"Baa."

"Right."

"Baa."

Our herd halts between four Quonset huts. The Sergeants line us up on the platoon street, a sidewalk that runs between the Quonset huts and the front lawns of dirt. They teach us to stand at attention. Stand tall and erect, as if a wire runs through our backs, pulls us straight up but not lift our feet off the deck, knees slightly bent, not locked. Heels touch, feet at a 45° angle. Shoulders back; chest out; stomach in; arms down our sides, straight, thumbs running down the sides of our legs; hands closed, but not like a fist, thumb on top of the U formed by index finger.

They show us how to make our racks. Tight hospital folds, smooth edges, tight surfaces. Tie our laundry bags to our racks, store all issued items; toiletries, laundry items, sundries.

On the platoon street, at attention, we wait for whatever comes next.

Maybe some sleep? I'm exhausted.

They instruct us on how to prepare for sleep. Show us how and where to stow our clothes after stripping down to our skivvies.

"STAND AT ATTENTION AT THE HEAD OF YOUR RACK. WHEN TOLD TO HIT THE RACK, YOU WILL JUMP INTO YOUR RACK BETWEEN THE SHEETS, REMAINING AT ATTENTION. YOU WILL NOT SLEEP UNTIL TOLD TO DO SO."

What?

"GO TO YOUR RACK. PREPARE FOR SLEEP."

We scramble to our racks, strip to skivvies, stow our clothes. Do not want to make a mistake. No telling what will happen.

When all is quiet, "HIT THE RACK!"

Huh?

Nobody in my hut moves. From the sound of things, nobody in the other huts move either. Too shell-shocked to move.

"HIT THE DAMN RACK!"

This time, we get it. Seventy-six recruits scramble into their racks. Get between the sheets.

Quiet.

A few seconds pass.

"REDDDDDEEEEE! SLEEP!"

Ooooohhhhh.

I survive my first day in the Marine Corps. A long one. Questions about myself and what is ahead, pop into my head. The beer and raucous night 24 hours ago catch up with me.

I thank my lucky stars. Time to get a good night's sleep.

Finally.

Quiet.

Sleep, restful, peaceful sleep.

Ahhhhhhhhh....

First Reveille

CRASH!

A trashcan careens through the hut, bounces off racks and footlockers. Bats, sticks, something, clangs on trashcan lids.

My eyelids pop open. I scramble out of my rack.

"GET THE HELL UP, MAGGOTS! OUT OF THOSE RACKS! MOVE IT, MAGGOTS! MOVE! MOVE! MOVE! MAKE YOUR RACKS. GET DRESSED. GET OUT! FALL IN ON THE PLATOON STREET. NOW! NOW! NOW!"

We dress.

"MOVE IT, PUKES!"

Make our racks.

"DO IT NOW! DO IT NOW! DO IT NOW!"

Crash through the hatches.

"FASTER! FASTER! FASTER!"

We spill out to the platoon street, scurry to our places. Come to attention. I look straight ahead at the guy across from me.

Do I look as ridiculous as he does?

Where hair once was, white sidewalls with cap resting on ears and eyebrows.

The Drill Instructor paces up and down the platoon street. He starts us off in a slow shuffle to the Mess Hall for breakfast.

Take All You Want
Eat All You Take

Reads the sign over the hatch of the Mess Hall.

"YOU WILL STEP TO THE TRAY RACK, TURN, FACE THE TRAYS, PLACE A HAND ON EACH SIDE OF THE TOP TRAY, LIFT IT, PLACE IT ON THE TRAY RAILS, PLACE A FORK AND KNIFE AND SPOON ON THE TRAY, HANDS ON THE TRAY, SIDESTEP DOWN THE CHOW LINE, YOU COME TO SOMETHING YOU WANT, LIFT THE TRAY UP CHIN HIGH, STRETCH YOUR ARMS OUT, AFTER THE FOOD IS PLACED ON YOUR TRAY, RETURN YOUR TRAY TO THE TRAY RAILS. CONTINUE DOWN THE CHOW LINE. WHEN FINISHED, STEP OVER TO ME."

Yes. Finally. We get to eat.

Speaking not a word, I pass on the oatmeal, get a tray full of scrambled eggs, bacon, hash browns, and toast, skip the S.O.S.

I step over to the Drill Instructor. Others follow. He stands at the head of a long table lined with a just—as—long wooden bench on each side. He points to a spot by the table.

With us lined up at the tables, trays in hand, he paces from the head of one table to another. Then, back.

"I SAY READY SEATS, YOU SIT.

"I SAY READY EAT, YOU EAT.

"DO YOU UNDERSTAND?"

"Yes, Sir!"

"REDEEEEEE, SEATS!"

We sit.

"GET UP! GET UP! GET UP!"

He paces.

"TOGETHER, GIRLS! WHEN I SAY SEATS I WANT TO HEAR SEVENTY-SIX ASSHOLES SUCKING WOOD! DO YOU UNDERSTAND?"

"YES, SIR!"

"REDEEEEEE, SEATS!"

It takes us several tries before we get it right.

"REDEEEEEE, EAT!"

We start.

"THAT'S ENOUGH! GET UP! GET UP! GET UP! GET OUT! GET OUT! GET OUT!"

He points to an exit.

Another Drill Instructor points where to empty our trays, toss our forks, knives, spoons, and trays.

Our third Drill Instructor forms us up.

My first day in the Marine Corps consists of 20 minutes sleep, a rude wake up, and a thirty second breakfast.

So, begins United States Marine Corps Boot Camp.

Squad Leader

BESIDES WRITTEN EXAMS, verbal quizzes on the platoon street are never ending. The fourth squad leader, my squad leader, cannot answer questions fast enough, if at all.

He is a good old boy from Arkansas. Not much on the uptake.

After two weeks of my squad leader screwing up drill and not doing well on the oral and written quizzes, "PRIVATE MORTON!"

"SIR! PRIVATE MORTON! AYE-AYE, SIR!"

What the...?

I double time to the platoon office. Knock three times on the hatch.

"I CAN'T HEAR YOU!"

I rap three times on the hatch.

"STILL CAN'T HEAR YOU!"

I pound three times on the hatch.

"ENTER!"

I remove my cover, march three steps in. Stop. Left face to the Drill Instructor's desk. "Sir, Private Morton reporting as ordered, Sir."

"You some sort of goddam genius?"

"No, Sir!"

"I think you are. You aced all the tests and quizzes."

What do I say to that? Nothing, stupid.

"Hamilton is dumber than dirt and can't drill worth a damn. Can you handle him?"

"Yes, Sir!"

"You sure?" Face close to mine.

Tom Morton

"Yes, Sir!"

"Good. You are my new fourth squad leader. Get out of here and send Hamilton in."

"Aye-Aye, Sir!"

With an inner smile, one step to the rear, left face. Three steps to the hatch. Replace cover. Exit. Sprint back to my squad bay.

"Hamilton, report to the platoon office."

"Who the hell do you think you are?"

"Your replacement."

"Your ass!"

He bolts up from his rack. Starts toward me.

This is gonna be fun!

Just in time from the platoon office, "PRIVATE HAMILTON!"

"SIR, PRIVATE HAMILTON! AYE-AYE, SIR!"

Hamilton glares at me. I grin. He clomps off.

What a dumb shit.

The Dentist Office

THE CORPSMAN LOOKS up at me from behind his desk. "Name?"

"Sir, Morton, Thomas D., Sir."

"Don't call me sir. You're next."

"Yes, Sir."

"Dammit, do not call me sir!"

Cranky.

I hear music on his radio, barely. My eyes glance down at the Corpsmen. I must look like I want to say something. Just above his desk, he wags his finger at me. He turns up the volume.

"....yellow submarine. We all live in a yellow submarine...."

I like it. I look down at him and raise my eyebrows.

He leans to look around me. In a voice I can barely hear, "Beatles. Yellow Submarine."

Not so cranky now. Must be the song.

From the dentist's office, "NEXT!"

10 Clicks

"PRIVATE MORTON!"

"SIR, PRIVATE MORTON. AYE-AYE, SIR!"

Three times I pound on the duty hut hatch.

"Enter."

I remove my cover. Three steps smartly in. Halt. Left face to the Drill Instructor's desk. Sergeant Peters stands behind it, arms folded across his chest.

"Sir, Private Morton reporting as ordered, Sir!"

"Taylor in your squad?"

"Yes, Sir!"

"Taylor doesn't know how to shave worth a crap. Your squad. Your responsibility. He will be clean shaven every morning. You know why?"

"No, Sir."

"Because you will shave him every morning. He will not have a hair, a stubble, not a whisker! Understand?"

"Yes, Sir!"

"Get out of here!"

"Aye-Aye, Sir!"

One step back, a sharp left face, three steps to the hatch, halt, return cover to gourd. Out the hatch. Double-time to my squad bay.

"Taylor!"

"What?" The mouse of few words replies.

"You will report to me every morning, in the head. I will shave you, every morning. You will not shave yourself. I will shave you. Understand?"

"Uh-huh." Says the mouse that will roar when he becomes a Marine.

Every morning I shave Taylor. He has not a hair, a whisker, a stubble. Nothing from the top of his ears, to below his T-shirt neckline, down his neck to his shoulders, all around his neck. Every morning I do all my squad leader duties, including my Taylor Task.

I don't have time to shave myself this morning,. *What the hell. No one will notice.*

As soon as we return from morning chow, "PRIVATE MORTON!"

"SIR! PRIVATE MORTON! AYE-AYE, SIR!"

Rush to the platoon office, up the three steps to the hatch, halt, and pound three times on the hatch frame.

"ENTER!"

I remove my cover. Three steps smartly in. Halt. Left face to the Drill Instructor's desk. Sergeant Peters sits behind it, glares at me. Sergeant Denally and Sergeant Rogers stand at each side of the desk, at ease. They look serious, stern.

"Sir, Private Morton reporting as ordered, Sir!"

"Did you shave this morning?" *Uh-oh.*

"Yes, Sir!"

"Are you sure?"

"Yes, Sir!" *Crap! Don't flinch, Morton. Keep eyes fixed.*

He gets up from his desk. Stalks around it. Positions himself close to my right. Ready to pounce. He leans in, his face nearly touches mine. "Very sure?"

"Yes, Sir!" *Stay with it, Morton!*

Whispers into my ear, "Come on, Morton. You can tell me. It'll be just between you and me. Our little secret."

He slides around to face me. We are almost nose to nose. His eyes burn into mine. A friendly grin on his face. "One more time. Did you shave this morning?"

Stick to it. Stick to it.

"Yes, Sir!"

He leans back. His eyes soften a little bit. His grin changes into a sly smile. He slips around to my left side. Whispers, "Then, I suggest you get 10 fucking clicks closer to the goddam razor blade from now on! Understand?"

"Yes, Sir!"

"Get your sorry unshaven ass out of my office!"

"Aye-Aye, Sir!"

I catch a glimpse of Denally and Rogers. They have the same sly look.

One step back, sharp left face, three steps to the hatch, halt, return cover to gourd.

"Sir, Gung-Ho, Sir!"

I, with my unshaven ass, flee the hell out of his office.

Wow! I'm still alive.

For the rest of boot camp I do get 10 fucking clicks closer to the goddam razor blade.

Mail Call

"FALL OUT FOR MAIL CALL!"

"SIR! FALL OUT FOR MAIL CALL! AYE-AYE, SIR!"

We double time onto the platoon street. Sergeant Peters sits on a stool at the head of the street. A mail bag rests on the deck to his left, a wastebasket to his right.

"I will call your name and hold up your mail in my fingertips. You will hustle up here like you want it. You will slap your hands together onto your mail. I will release your mail. And then you will double-time back to your place, holding your mail between your hands. You will hold your mail until told to open it. Do you understand?"

"YES, SIR!"

Mail. Letters from home. From Karen.

"BASKERVILLE!"

Baskerville hustles up the platoon street, like he wants it, gets to the Sergeant, but he holds Baskerville's mail away from him. Hands apart, waist high, ready to retrieve his mail, he appears stunned, doesn't know what to do. He freezes.

"You a hound, Baskerville?"

"No, Sir." Still frozen.

"With a name like Baskerville you must be." A small smile on Sergeant Peter's face.

"No, Sir." Has not moved.

The second his mail is lowered to between his hands, Baskerville slaps them together on the envelope, scurries back to his place. His mail between his hands, held chest high, looks as if he is praying for something good in the envelope.

The Sergeant looks as if he is chuckling to himself as he looks down at the mail in his hand.

"GROUT!" All business now.

Same action.

"JENKINS!"

Same thing.

The Sergeant pauses. Feels the next envelope. "What do we have here? Gum?

"BARNES!"

Barnes, hustles up the platoon street, like he wants it, gets to the Sergeant, slaps his hands together for the envelope. Sergeant Peters snaps it away at the last second. Smiles.

"You will take your mail and stay here."

"Aye-Aye, Sir!"

The Sergeant holds up the envelope. Barnes slaps it away. Stands there.

"Open it."

"Sir. Open it. Aye-Aye, Sir."

Barnes does.

"Remove the gum, unwrap it, throw the wrapper in here." He holds up the wastebasket.

Barnes unwraps the gum, throws the wrapper into the wastebasket.

"Put the gum into your mouth."

Barnes pops gum goes into mouth.

"Chew."

Barnes' jaw moves.

"Spit it out!" Raises the wastebasket to Barnes' chin.

The gum rockets out of his mouth.

CLUNK.

"That's all, Barnes. Get back there."

The look on Barnes face shows his disappointment.

Sergeant Peters doles out more mail.

"RICHARDS!"

Richards does the routine, except he clips the Sergeant's fingers. He bolts upright, "AARRRGGGGHHH!"

Richards stands there, leans back, mail in his hands.

The Sergeant circles around him.

"Don't you ever touch me again! Understand?"

"Yes, Sir!"

"Hit the deck and give me twenty-five!"

"Aye-Aye, Sir." Richards starts his twenty-five push-ups.

"One, Sir.

"Two, Sir.

"Three, Sir...."

Mail call resumes until, "Twenty-five, Sir." Richards gets to his feet.

"Pick up your mail and get back in formation."

"Aye-Aye, Sir!"

The Drill Instructor holds up a package. Shakes it.

"Ahh, cookies.

"DIXON!"

Dixon double times up the platoon street, not so much like he wants it, more like he knows something will happen. Stops in front of the Sergeant, at attention.

"Take it and stay here. Be careful. Don't break the cookies."

"Aye-Aye, Sir."

He hands the package to Dixon. "Open it."

"Sir. Open it. Aye-Aye, Sir."

Dixon opens it.

The Sergeant takes the box. Sniffs the contents. "Hmmm. Wonderful. Pass one out to everybody."

"Sir. Pass one out to everybody. Aye-Aye, Sir."

Dixon does. Finished, he hands the package to the Sergeant. He throws the package, with the rest of the cookies, into the wastebasket. Dixon doesn't get a cookie.

"READY. EAT!"

"SIR. EAT. AYE-AYE, SIR."

We eat.
Oh, man, chocolate chip!

Mail call over, we return to our squad bays. Read our mail.
My next letter home begins,
Dear Mom,
Please don't send me anything in the mail….

Fly Bye

ON THE PLATOON street, Sergeant Peters explains how medals and awards are earned.

"The Good...."

A loud noise from the air drowns him out.

The source, a helicopter, circles above us. Then departs.

"The Good Conduct...."

The helicopter returns. Seems louder.

Sergeant Peters glares at it.

I bite my lip to keep from laughing out loud.

It hovers longer than last time before it flies away.

He resumes.

The helicopter. Again.

Internal laughter shakes my insides.

Sergeant Peters extends his arms at the helicopter. Waves them back and forth.

"GET THE FUCK OUTTA HERE!"

Yeah. Like that's gonna work.

It leaves, engine noise fades away.

Are you shitting me?

"The Good Conduct Medal is for three years of undetected crime."

Undetected crime? Hmmm.

Midnight Business

A BUTTON COMES off one of my shirts. Before lights out, I gather my Marine Corps issued sewing kit, the shirt, and a button. I stick them under my pillow for easy access in the dark. Prepared to do the necessary repair, ready for the command to hit the rack.

Command given. Into my rack. Wait for Taps.

After Taps, "**GOOD NIGHT CHESTY PULLER WHEREVER YOU ARE!**"

"**SIR, GOOD NIGHT CHESTY PULLER WHEREVER YOU ARE, AYE-AYE, SIR!**"

Now.

Hop out of my rack, put on shower shoes, grab shirt, button and sewing kit. Creep off to the head.

Doing my business, I begin sewing a button onto my shirt. Out of the corner of my eye, in the hatch, appears Sergeant Peters, the Senior Drill Instructor. He wears Drill Instructor Casual Evening Wear; Smokey Bear Cover, Marine Corps Bulldog Tee Shirt, Khaki Trousers with duty belt.

Shit!

I should shout "ten-hut!" And jump to attention. I sit on the crapper, skivvies around my ankles, in mid-stitch, taking a dump.

Whadda I do? What the hell do I do?

I turn my head to face him. Our eyes lock. In one swift motion, he snaps his right hand up into the stop position, purses his lips, turns his eyes down, does a sharp left face, disappears from the hatch.

What a relief! Wait. Was that a hint of a smile I saw when he turned and walked away? Found it funny? Sense of humor?

Mess and Maintenance Week

HALFWAY THROUGH BOOT camp my platoon leads the competitions. Blew out three other platoons in close order drill, academics, physical training. As the top platoon, Sergeant Peters gets first choice as to what our assignment will be for Mess and Maintenance Week. He opts for maintenance. A reward from him to us for being top platoon. It is a no pressure week for us. This assignment assures we will be more rested than the other platoons for the following two weeks to qualify with the M14 at Edson Range.

Assigned to a warehouse, I hand out uniforms to recruits further along into boot camp than me. Corporal Jones is in charge. Just him and me in the warehouse.

I stand behind the counter, by myself. The Corporal busies himself in his office. His radio blares out a Top 40 hit.

Three silhouettes appear in the doorway. Backlit by the sun. They enter the dimly lit warehouse. The next things I see, the only things I see, are the two stars on the collar of the first silhouette.

I snap to attention, salute. "Sir, good morning, Sir."

He returns my salute. "Good morning, Private. What's your name?"

"Sir, Private Morton, Thomas D., Sir."

"Do you know who I am?"

"Yes, Sir. Major General Hochmuth, Commanding General, MCRD, San Diego. Sir."

"Are you here by yourself, Private Morton?"

"No, Sir."

"Who else is here?"

"Sir, Corporal Jones, Sir."

"Where is Corporal Jones?"

"Sir, Corporal Jones is in his office, Sir."

"I see."

He starts back to the Corporal's office. *Oops.*

"At ease, Private." I comply. But, I am not.

Hold your nose, Jones. You're in deep shit.

Radio goes silent. One voice, the General's, quiet but stern, chews out Jones. The voice so low, I can't make out what he says.

The General exits the office. Corporal Jones follows.

Back to attention.

"Your place is out here, Corporal. You stay out here." The General sounds miffed.

"Yes, Sir!"

"Carry on."

"Sir, Aye-Aye, Sir!"

The General strides out the doorway, a silhouette once again, then vanishes.

Holy crap. The General.

Chow on the Range

TODAY WILL BE a long one. It is the first day of live firing on the rifle range. Qualifying week. An important week.

Zero-dark-thirty. We go through the chow line.

At the scrambled eggs station, I hold out my tray. The recruit serving the eggs plops half a serving onto my tray.

"More."

"Move on." *Jeez.*

I do. *Don't hold up the line.*

To the hash browns station. Same thing.

"More."

"Keep moving." *Again?*

Bacon next.

"More."

"No. Keep moving." *This ain't right.*

At our dining table, I stand at attention, tray in hands. Peak down at the meager meal that is supposed to carry me to noon chow. I want more. I need more.

The rest of my squad lines up next to me. I see they have small portions, too. We are far enough away from Sergeant Rogers, I know he can't hear me.

I whisper to Ponce, "You want more?"

"Yeah."

I figure the rest of the squad does, as well.

I step over to Sergeant Rogers.

"Sir, the Private requests permission to speak, Sir."

"Speak."

I stretch my arms out, give him a good look at what is on my tray.

"Sir, is this all the Private is to subsist on, Sir?"

He glowers down at my tray. "Did you ask for more?"

"Yes, Sir."

"Others want more?"

"Yes, Sir."

"Come with me."

"Aye-Aye, Sir."

I follow him to our table.

"Platoon 2082. For more chow fall in behind Private Morton."

As they start to fall in behind me, "Come with me, Private Morton."

I follow him to the head of the chow line. He confers with another Drill Instructor, who turns to the line that is about to start through. "Platoon. Halt." They do.

Sergeant Rogers turns to me. "Fall in line, Private Morton."

I do.

He turns to the servers. "You will give these people as much as they ask for. Understand?"

A chorus of, "Yes, Sir!"

"Carry on, Private Morton."

"Aye-Aye, Sir."

I hold out my tray to the server. No problem this time. A large portion of scrambled eggs is plunked on my tray. I continue through the chow line, followed by the rest of my squad and then, the rest of the platoon. We get all the chow we want.

At our table, at attention, ready for the dining routine.

Sergeant Rogers steps up to the head of our table. He turns his head toward me. My eyes move to look at him. Our eyes meet. I give him an ever so slight nod. He does the same.

"Ready. Seats."

Our butts, all together, hit the benches.

"Ready. Eat."

No hesitation on our parts.

A good breakfast. Spirits soar. To the range with our M14s.

The Toilet Seat

WE HAVE TWO weeks to qualify with the M14 to meet Marine Corps standards for shooting. It is the first true step to become a Marine.

First week, we snap in, learn BRASS, dry fire in various positions; offhand, kneeling, sitting, and prone. And, proper use of the rifle sling for support and stability while shooting.

The second week, we live fire. My shooting indicates I will qualify Expert.

Wednesday night, the week of qualifying, "PRI I I I VATE MORTON!"

"SIR! PRI I I I VATE MORTON! AYE-AYE, SIR!"

I double time to the duty hut, do the routine, then Sergeant Peters does his routine.

I stand tall at attention in front of his desk. "Sir, Private Morton reporting as ordered, Sir!"

"You shot expert today?"

"Yes, Sir!"

"You know what Taylor shot?"

"No, Sir!"

"He shot shit! At this rate he won't qualify. He don't qualify, we don't have 100% qualified. We will have 100% qualified in this platoon. He's in your squad. You will see to it that he does qualify."

What?

"He will be next to you on the firing line. After each shot, you will check his score. For every Maggie's drawers, you will tell him to shoot his next shot at your target. And you will shoot at his target. Understand?"

"Yes, Sir!"

"You will both qualify. We will have 100% qualified for this platoon. We will be the honor platoon. Dismissed!"

"Aye-Aye, Sir!"

Our platoon qualifies 100%.

Taylor and I qualify as Marksman.

The Marksman Badge is referred to as The Toilet Seat.

Sergeant Peters' Three Pleasures

0430

PT, live fire on the range, more PT, run, more PT. A long day on the range.

We stand at order arms outside the squad bay. Grimy. Sweaty. Tired. Wait to be dismissed.

Sergeant Peters appears on the second floor stairwell balcony. He wears his Smokey Bear cover, a short sleeve USMC sweatshirt, sleeves split so his arms can fit through. Dress trousers and duty belt. In one hand, a cup of coffee, in the other, a lit cigar. Sergeant Peters looks down at us, sips his coffee.

"UP AND ON SHOULDERS. FOUR COUNT EXERCISE, CADENCE COUNT, I WILL COUNT, FOORRRRR, EVVVVERRRRR!"

Oh, bitchin. Just fucking bitchin.

A billow of blue-gray smoke swirls up and away from a puff of his cigar.

"REDDD EEEEE, BEGIN. ONE, TWO, THREE."

"ONE!"

"ONE, TWO, THREE."

"TWO!"

"ONE, TWO, THREE."

"THREE!"

"PLAH, TOON, COUNT."

"FOUR!"

"COUNT!"

"TWO! THREE! FIVE!

"ONE! TWO! THREE! SIX!

"ONE! TWO! THREE! SEVEN!"

We count. He sips his coffee, puffs on his cigar. He looks as if he enjoys what he sees.

At 900, "SIGH, LENT, COUNT."

"901."

"COUNT!"

Two, three, 902.

One, two, three, 903.

Another swirl of smoke. Another sip of coffee.

"I HAVE THREE PLEASURES IN LIFE. KNOW WHAT THEY ARE?"

More smoke. More coffee.

"DRINKING!"

906.

"FUCKING!"

907.

"AND OBSERVING PAIN! GUESS WHICH ONE I'M DOING RIGHT NOW!"

His thunderous growl-laugh sounds humorously evil. Returns his cigar to his mouth, tilts his head back, looks like FDR. Smoke spirals around him, up into the air.

910.

One, two, three, 911.

One, two, three, 912.

"LET ME HEAR YOU!"

"913!"

"One, Two, Three, 914!

"One, Two, Three, 915!

"One, Two, Three, 916!"

Twelve hundred reps make for a sound sleep.

Hygiene Inspection

WE STAND BAREFOOT, in skivvies, on our footlockers, heels above the lock clasp.

Sergeant Peters comes by to check for heel contusions, blisters, and other foot and ankle problems. Then an about-face. He checks my toes, insteps, and arches.

Finishes with me, he turns to go to the next guy. Stops. Returns. He looks me in the face, looks down at my feet, then back up at me. "Those are some god-dam wide feet. You must've been barefoot all your life. Never had a pair shoes. Were you some sort of barefoot, outback-woods Okie?"

"No, Sir!"

He looks at my feet, then back up at me. "You're shittin' me. Those ain't natural. Those things are wide. You sure they're feet?"

"Yes, Sir!"

He looks at my feet, back up at me, at my feet again, then looks me straight in the eye. "They used to be flippers, right?"

"No, Sir!"

Still looks me straight in the eye, "One of those damn long-haired surfer bums, always barefoot, weren't you?"

"No, Sir!" *Damn! How'd he figure that out?*

He shakes his head. Turns to walk away. Takes two steps.

Jeez.

Then, he back steps to me.

Damn.

Looks at my feet, then up at me. "You had webs between your toes. Didn't you? You had webs between your toes and you cut 'em out just so you could get into my Marine Corps. Didn't you?"

"No, Sir!"

He turns to walk away, again. He gets to the next guy.

Finally.

Turns around, returns to me.

Shit!

He looks down at my feet. Again. Back up at me. Again. "I've seen a lot of feet in my day. Them's some goddam wide dawgs! Know what I'm saying?"

"Yes, Sir!"

He half smiles. Looks at my feet, shakes his head, moves on to the next guy.

At last.

I almost laugh. Glad I hold it back.

Sergeant Rogers'
Promotion

CONFIDENCE BUILDS IN me, in all of us. A sense, a feeling.

We are becoming Marines.

Pride settles in.

Halfway through boot camp, the in-your-face business is almost over. Don't get things correct, perfect, the in-your-face thunders down. None of us wants that ever again.

Sergeant Rogers marches us to class. Runs us through close order drills. He calls out, "Delayed cay-dence, Count!"

At the proper time, on cue, all of us in unison, do the delayed cadence.

One, two, three, "ONE!"

One, two, three, "TWO!"

One, two, three, "THREE!"

One, two, three, "FOUR!"

One, "ONE!"

Two, "TWO!"

Three, "THREE!"

Four, "FOUR!"

"ONE, TWO, THREE, FOUR, WE LOVE THE MARINE CORPS!"

Sergeant Rogers, in his kindest drill instructor voice, "You may have noticed that I call you...." A few steps, then, "girls. Once you get squared away, I will call you...." Our steps get crisper, we stand taller, chests stick out more, shoulders square back more. We can hardly wait for what he is about to say. "LADIES! Arup, tu, tree, fo!"

I can almost hear us think at the same time. *Shit.*

Sergeant Rogers grins like a madman, on the inside. I just know it.

"Arup, tu, tree, fo! Arup, tu, tree, fo!"

Platoon 2082 continues on, still Girls but soon to be Ladies.

We are so proud.

Hand-to-Hand

"GIVE ME A volunteer!

"You! Maggot! Get up here!"

Crap.

I scramble up onto the platform, stand at attention on the spot he indicates.

"I will demonstrate one way to get out of a choke hold."

He steps in front of me. Turns his back to me.

"Grab me around the throat, in a choke hold."

I reach up and do so.

He snarls, "ARGHHHHHH!"

I am airborne over his shoulder. Slam into the deck. Thanks to judo lessons as a kid, the air stays in my lungs. His hand hammers down to crush my throat, stops at the last instant.

He stomps all over the platform, snorts like an angry bull. His eyes on fire, his face contorts.

Pleeeeeeeeeeease, don't stomp me!

"On your feet!"

Once again, I stand at attention on the spot he indicates.

He steps to the front of me, again.

Oh, crap, crap, crap!

"Try again, stupid!" Turns his back to me.

Here we go.

This time, up on my toes, I reach around to put a choke hold on him, without touching him.

Again, airborne, slam into the deck, his hand hammers toward my throat, stops short.

His face looks different. Determined, not angry. Determined to finish the job, to kill me, the enemy.

"When you throw your man down, keep your grip on his arm with one hand and slam the other hand down through his throat into the deck."

End of first lesson on hand-to-hand combat.

Bayonet Training

ANOTHER BUSY DAY, but with some fun.

Charge stuffed dummies. Slash and stab them with the bayonet attached to my rifle.

As we march to the platoon street, I recall the crucial words barked out by the bayonet training instructor.

"A bayonet is six inches long. It takes only two inches to kill a man. The Marine Corps gives you four extra inches to fuck around with."

Yeah. Bet it's more fun using all six inches.

Junk on the Bunk

AFTER EVENING CHOW, Sergeant Peters teaches us how to put the junk on the bunk. He sets a bunk out on the platoon street. Places an item on the bunk.

"Quickly, people! GO!"

We rush into our squad bays, to our bunks, place the same item on our bunks. Rush back out onto the platoon street to find out what the next item is and where to place it.

It is back and forth, back and forth.

As squad leader, it is my responsibility to make sure everybody follows the instructions and gets back out to the platoon street without delay.

See an item placed on the bunk, run to place the item on our bunks, run back out for the next item.

Pressure builds. Ingram does not start back to the platoon street.

"Get out there!"

"Fuck you!"

I grab him. Throw him out the hatch. I follow. He turns, comes at me. My punch crushes his nose, knocks him back onto his ass.

The end? Nope. End of round one.

He scrambles up. Comes at me again. Another smash to his nose sends him to the deck a second time. End of round two.

He rises up to begin round three. Before he gets to me, before I put him on his ass again, my feet fly off the deck. Ingram and me, eye to eye, my nose to his bleeding nose, Sergeant Peters hurls us through the hatch into the squad bay.

"Get this settled then get your asses back out here!" Turns, storms out to the platoon street.

"Had enough?"

"Yeah," Ingram snorts.

Blood covers his lips and chin.

With my sleeve, I wipe the blood from his face. Back out to the platoon street for more junk on the bunk instruction.

Sergeant Peters looks up at us. Smiles. Resumes his instructions.

We do the same.

The Smoking Lamp

WE STAND AT ease on the platoon street.

Sergeant Denally smiles, bellows, "THE SMOKING LAMP IS LIT FOR ONE CIGARETTE!"

"SIR, THE SMOKING LAMP IS LIT FOR ONE CIGARETTE, AYE-AYE, SIR!"

The smokers smoke 'em if they got 'em. I am not and do not.

While the smoking lamp is lit, I do nothing, just stand around, look stupid. Keller always offers me a cigarette. I decline, always.

I decide to try smoking. I accept Keller's offer and light up.

First drag gags me. I swallow it. No need to draw attention.

Finished, we field strip the cigarette and put the kotex in our pockets for later disposal.

Keller welcomes me into the smokers' world. I am one of the guys, a smoker. No longer will I do nothing when the smoking lamp is lit.

I'll quit smoking after boot camp.

The Sandwich

THE END COMES into view. Three weeks left. Our Drill Instructors push us to perfect everything; PT, military knowledge, Marine Corp history, close order drill. In preparation for final competitions and inspections. We are close to officially being Marines. Our three Sergeants treat us as such.

Before noon chow, "PRIVATE MORTON!"

"SIR! PRIVATE MORTON! AYE-AYE, SIR!"

Double time to the Drill Instructors' office. Follow entry protocol. It never changes.

"Sir! Private Morton reporting as ordered, Sir!"

"We're about to go to chow. I forgot my lunch today. Roast beef is being served. There's fries, too. Bring me back a roast beef sandwich and fries. Understand?" Sergeant Peters asks with a sly twinkle in his eyes.

"Yes, Sir. Anything else, Sir?"

A smile, "I like mustard on my sandwich and catsup with my fries. Go get it."

"Aye-Aye, Sir!" Execute the exit routine.

To the Mess Hall.

Chow gobbled down, I turn to Miller. "Take my tray."

He looks at me as if I'm crazy.

"Just do it."

He puts my tray under his.

I return to the chow line, get another tray, load up on roast beef, bread, fries, and napkins.

Miller gawks at me as I sit. "What the hell are you doing?"

"Don't sweat it."

"If you say so."

Make the sandwich, wrap it up in napkins, stuff it into my shirt. Same with the fries.

Exit the Mess Hall. I turn in my second tray. Stroll back into the Mess Hall. Wander over to the condiment table. Look around, check the coast. It is clear. I drop a jar of mustard down my trousers' left leg. My bloused trousers keep the jar from crashing onto the deck. I look around again. All clear. Next, a bottle of catsup finds its way down my trousers' right leg.

Into formation. March back to the platoon area.

"PRIVATE MORTON!"

"SIR! PRIVATE MORTON! AYE-AYE, SIR!"

Execute the routine. Enter the office. Sergeant Peters sits behind his desk, leans back, hands clasped behind his head.

"Sir, Private Morton...."

"Yeah. Yeah. Yeah. Well?" He sits up.

I reach into my shirt, pull out the sandwich. Put it on his desk.

"Good." A smirk crosses his face. "And?"

I do the same with the fries.

His smirk becomes a smile.

I unbuckle my belt.

"Whoa! Hold on there!"

He looks dumbfounded. Stands up.

"Sir, a moment, Sir."

I unbutton my trousers.

"What the hell do you think you're doing?" Dumfounded changes to alarmed.

I reach down into my trousers' legs. Pull out the mustard and catsup, one at a time.

Smack them onto his desk.

He laughs, "Excellent. Button up and get out!"

"Aye-Aye, Sir!"

I button up, buckle up, and get out.

Graduation

"EYE—DOUGH—LAYO—ITE—LAYO!

"EYE—DOUGH—LAYO—ITE—LAYO!"

His cadence strong, clear, and filled with pride, Sergeant Peters marches us across the parade ground. His Platoon, Platoon 2082, the Honor Platoon, my Platoon, steps smartly for its graduation ceremony at the front of the base theater.

The proper dignitaries speak about the training we go through and how proud everybody should be. Sweat from the morning sun beating down on me slides down my face, neck, back. I don't care. Let me out of the sun. I need to see Karen, hold her, kiss her sweet lips.

Finally, Sergeant Peters does an about-face, his NCO sword at his right shoulder. He salutes with his sword and bellows, "PLATOON TWO THOUSAND EIGHTY-TWO, DISMISSED!"

Loud and clear, in unison, perfect harmony, unlike that first day, "SIR, PLATOON TWO THOUSAND EIGHTY-TWO, DISMISSED! AYE-AYE, SIR!"

One step to the rear.

"GUNG HO!"

About-face and we scatter to join family and friends. With a couple hours of base liberty, we may go anywhere within the confines of MCRD, but must return to the platoon street by 1600.

Smiles fill everyone's faces. New Marines, their families and friends. Tears stream down some.

There she is!

A big grin on her face, Karen runs to me almost as fast as I run to her. We hug for not long enough. We kiss. A kiss saying more than glad to see you.

I notice my parents. A handshake from Dad, with the expected, "I'm proud of you, son."

A hug from Mom, "Congratulations, Tommy." She runs her hand down my tie.

At the snack-bar, I gobble down hamburgers, French fries, ice cream, and all the other things I did without during boot camp. Time is short. I make the most of it. Enjoy every second.

All too soon, I am back on the platoon street. One more night at MCRD before BIT at Camp Pendleton, just up the coast.

We can't cure the incurable, raise the dead, feed hundreds with one fish and a loaf of bread, turn water into wine, walk on water, or rise from the dead. But, we are as perfect as our Drill Instructors, our idols, our gods on earth, could make us.

We understand.

It is a perfect day.

It is official.

We are United States Marines.

Before Viet Nam

Fire Watch

AT CAMP PENDLETON we put in long, hard hours. Training starts at first light. Ends after sunset. Sometimes lasts overnight.

Back at the barracks each night:

Priority one; peel off sweat-soaked, dirt-caked, grime-smeared utilities.

Priority two; get to the shower before the hot water runs out, scrub off the dirt and grime.

Dead tired after a hard day out in the field, the barracks buzzes, everyone does the same thing at the same time. Try to clean up. A tired, sore man stands under each showerhead. Steam billows out from the ache relieving hot water.

"PVT. ALLEN, TO THE DUTY DESK ON THE DOUBLE!"

"SIR! PVT. ALLEN, TO THE DUTY DESK ON THE DOUBLE! AYE-AYE, SIR!"

A few minutes later, Allen struts tall and proud, through the barracks, wet from his interrupted shower. Wears nothing but a helmet liner and shower shoes. In one hand he twirls a lanyard attached to a whistle. With the other hand, he thumps his thigh with a nightstick. He looks vigilant and cocky.

"Hey! Allen! Whaddaya gonna do if there's a fire? Piss on it?"

He nods.

I feel safe. I am sure everyone does.

First Leave

BIT FINISHES, TIME to leave Camp Pendleton. Get my first leave underway. Thirty days. Then, report to MCRD, San Diego for Radio Telegraph Operator School. Whatever the hell that is.

Who knows where next? Viet Nam? Probably. For now, pack my sea bag. Find my way home.

The base shuttle takes a bunch of us to the Greyhound bus depot, Oceanside. A bank of phones catches my eye. *Call Mom.*

"Hi, Mom.

"Yes. Everything's fine.

"Really.

"I got thirty days leave.

"Can you pick me up at Greyhound downtown?

"Sixteen hundred hours.

"Sorry, Mom. Four o'clock.

"Yeah. Thanks.

"Love you, too. Bye."

An hour to kill before the next bus to San Diego. Enough time to make another call.

"Hello, ma'am. This is Tom. May I speak to Karen?

"Yes, thank you, ma'am."

Come on, come on.

"Hey, babe!

"You're damn right it's your Tom-Tom.

"Oh, you don't know how much I missed you, too. Or how much I love you.

"Thirty days.

"Tonight.

"Oh, I don't know. Movie, submarine races?

"Yeah. Both work for me, too.

"Nineteen hundred hours. Sorry. Seven o'clock. My mom's picking me up.

"I know. Me, too. Sorry. I just thought it better this way. Have dinner with her. Get it out of the way. Besides, my car is there.

"Yup. I'll pick you up at seven.

"I love you more.

"Yes, I do.

"Uh-huh.

"Okay. Okay. Okay. You win. I'll see you at seven. I love you so much.

"Okay. Bye."

The call for boarding the express bus to San Diego resounds as music for my ears. The seat at the rear offers no comfort. But, it will do just fine. It takes me to thirty days of freedom. And Karen.

Cruise down I-5 for a shade over an hour, we arrive in downtown San Diego. Get off the bus, retrieve my sea bag, hoist it onto my shoulder, zigzag through the crowd.

Out of the way, people.

Outside, the cool, clean air feels good.

I find Mom. She opens the trunk.

"It's good to have you home, Tommy."

Sea bag in the trunk. Big mom-son hug.

"Thanks, Mom. Good to be home."

We hop into the car.

Mom negotiates her way through downtown rush hour traffic to G St., onto Highway 94, to Lemon Grove, and home. 2446 Bonita St.

My sisters, Val and Candy, and baby brother, Nino, greet me with ohs, ahs, and hugs.

Must be the uniform. Enjoy it now. Won't be on for long.

"Hi. Hi. And, hi. Come on, guys. Let me change."

"Okay, but hurry. Dinner's ready. Your clothes are in your closet."

"Thanks, Mom."

White Levis and tan T-shirt hang on me. My belt, now too long, underscores my forty pounds shed. My Marine Corps web belt, cut to the correct length, does the trick. Cinches up my Levis. My untucked T-shirt covers it up. Splash on some Hai Karate. I am ready for action.

Aromas from the kitchen caress me. Invite me.

Home. Mom's cooking. Not mess hall chow.

The dining room table looks wonderful, right out of Better Homes and Gardens. Mom's good china, fancy silverware, and the fine crystal glasses make a welcome table setting. The food, the steam rising. Plates, not stainless steel trays.

"Let's eat."

Fried chicken. Drumsticks and thighs for me, stacked high on a platter. Drop one of each onto my plate.

Green beans fill a huge bowl. I heap a large serving onto my plate, drown them in butter.

Another bowl holds rice. A heap of that. Again, the butter.

Ice cold milk from a Miller's Dairy half-gallon glass bottle.

My first home cooked meal since before boot camp. Too good.

Food constantly in my mouth prevents me from saying much. Grunts, a few yups, some nods and shakes of my head. And glances at the clock. Too many glances.

"Going somewhere, Tommy?"

Jeez, Mom. You miss nothing, do you. "Yup."

"Karen?"

A couple nods. *Who'd you think?*

The food once on my plate, disappears faster than it should. Seeing Karen, being with her takes precedence now. I did my son's duty.

"Gotta go." I start for the door.

"Tommy."

"What?"

She comes up to me, hugs me. "Be careful."

"Yes, ma'am."

To the car.

To Karen.

To my love.

Her house looks the same. Just as I ring the doorbell, the door opens. Karen stands there, a sight for my sore eyes. Light brown, almost blond, hair a perfect page boy. Big brown eyes radiate love, warmth, with a twinkle of mischief. A smile of perfectly straight teeth that shine a brilliant white. Her face, her demeanor, hide no mystery. An open book.

She turns her head, bids her parents good night. Muffled replies.

She steps out. Closes the door. Her arm in my arm, she pulls me close. We stroll out to the car.

She whispers in my ear, "I don't think I can sit through a movie. And I don't want to, either." *Outstanding.*

"A-Okay with me."

She giggles. *Out-fucking-standing.*

Her perfume, soft and sweet, tells me I am truly home. Heightens the expectations for the evening.

Before I start the car, she starts me up with a hard, hot, down-my-throat kiss.

Kiss ends. With a gasp for breath, I blurt, "Let's go."

We are off to the submarine races.

The first race starts before we get into the gate. She is half way over the seat, on her way to the padded roomy back of my station wagon. The race begins with me grabbing her from behind.

Each race is fast and furious. Some sprints, some routes. Ample down time between races provides adequate rest between races.

Races over, participants spent, I take her home. The first light of day pushes the last darkness of night. The afterglow of love surrounds us.

I walk her to the door. A light glows through the cute, flower print curtains of the kitchen window. Her parents await.

"You'll be ok?"

"Sure. Why not?"

"Your parents."

"I can handle them. Ok?"

"Ok."

She lays another kiss on me. A long, lingering kiss. As good as the one at the beginning of the evening. Savory. With staying power. Then, ends, ever so slowly.

She touches her forehead to mine.

"Welcome home, my Tom-Tom. I love you."

"I love you."

A quick peck on my cheek. She opens the screen door. I hold it open while she unlocks the front door. The click sounds like a pop. She opens the door a crack, turns her head back to me, eyes mischievously bright. "See you later?"

"Of course. Got some things to do first."

"Call me when you're done."

She flashes another one of her joyous, light-up-the-universe smiles. She opens the door. Creeps in. Her parents stand at the end of the hallway. They do not look happy.

Am I still so tan I should be at the back door?

Karen eases the door shut.

I walk down the gaily-colorful flower-lined path. Voices from the house drift out to me.

They are not happy voices.

Good luck.

Into my car. Head home.

Radio School

I NOW KNOW what radio school is. My effort to be different than my dad fails. I am in radio school, Radio Telegraph Operator School. Learn Morse code. Tap out messages on a telegraph key. Type incoming messages, at twenty words a minute. Like my dad in 1943.

With less than six months in the Marine Corps, pay is low. Being poor, my classmates live on base. I can afford to live off base because I live with my mother, rent free. Plus, I get commrats.

The first weeks of school are in an enclosed room. The keys for tapping out Morse code blast out the dits and dahs. The sound reverberates around the room, bounces off the walls, into our heads, where they bounce around quicker and louder. No one escapes the headaches.
>   Di dah dah dah
>   Di dah dah dah
>   Di dah dah dah
>   Morse code for J, the first letter we learn. Repeated over and over and over. School is difficult.

Middle of the night, the phone rings.
>   A knock on my bedroom door.
>   "Tommy, it's for you."
>   "Who is it, Mom?"
>   "I don't know. He asked for PFC Morton." *Now what?*

My head pounds. I put the phone to my ear.

"PFC Morton, Sir."

A falsetto voice, "di di di dit di dit di di dit dah dah dah dah dit."

"Ha, ha, Dad."

"I thought you'd like that." He chuckles. "Got a headache do you?"

"Yeah."

"It'll go away in about a week."

"Gee, thanks for the good news."

"You're welcome. Hit the rack, jarhead!"

"Aye-Aye, squid!"

A laugh, then dial tone.

Funny, Dad, very funny.

My headache and I go back to bed. Zero-dark-thirty, comes fast.

0700

We take our seats. Sergeant Pearson begins his lecture on radio procedure.

0735

He goes silent. Gazes to the back of the room. I turn to see what he sees.

Lueck, leaning back in his chair, face toward the ceiling, asleep.

I look back at the Sergeant. He tosses his one and a half-inch diameter chalk up and down with his hand. Then, throws it.

I turn in time to see Lueck flip backwards, hands and feet flailing in the air, then disappear. In nothing flat, he jumps to his feet, picks up his chair, sits down. A large bump forms in the middle of his forehead.

Sergeant Pearson picks up another piece of chalk from his desk. Continues his lecture.

Do not doze off in class.

TJ

THE GUYS ASK me where to meet girls and dance. They believe I know some secret because I am from San Diego. I tell them if what they want is a good time, dance and drink, there is only one place. Oscar's in TJ.

"Isn't it dangerous down there?"

"It's safe, if you behave yourself. And, stay out of the dives. It's totally safe at Oscar's. I've been going there since I was 16. Girls not old enough to drink up here, go down there. Some local chicks go there, as well. It's always packed. Booze is cheap, beer cheaper."

We make plans to go Saturday night.

Six of us pile into my car. Bug out for TJ. Final stop, Oscar's. Daniels, his car full, follows me.

At Oscar's, we drink ourselves silly. Dance our asses off.

At 0400, as agreed, we rendezvous at the cars for the trip back to the base. Daniels is nowhere to be found. The guys from his car say they will wait for him. My guys and I leave.

Monday morning Daniels is AWOL. No one knows where he is. The guys from his car say he never showed up at Oscar's or his car. At sun-up, they took a cab to the border, walked across. Took a cab to the base.

Radio school continues. Without Lance Corporal Michael Daniels.

1967

General Lunch

EVERYONE TIRES OF mess hall chow. The PX snack bar serves good burgers and fries.

Payday blesses us with money to burn on good food. As soon as morning class ends, we hustle off to snag an All-American lunch. Could run into some girls.

A basket, with a cheeseburger and overflowing fries, sits on my tray. My Coke has no lid, no straw. I drink it like a man, straight out of the cup. Best meal of the day until I gobble down a home cooked Mom-meal. Nordstrom and Kretowicz motion me over to their table.

The usual bullshit starts before my butt hits the chair.

"What'd you do last weekend?"

"Met me a girl."

"The surf was ratty. Not much to enjoy. Maybe next weekend. It's gotta get better."

"Ain't the water cold?"

"I wear a wetsuit, numb-nuts."

"What's with Sergeant Hines? We do nothing good enough for him."

"What a prick."

"Yeah. A real dickhead."

On and on and on. All the while, we woof down burgers and fries. Suck in Cokes and shakes.

"I'm getting an ice cream cone. I'll meet you guys outside."

Vanilla cone in hand, I meet up with Nordstrom and Kretowicz. A couple other guys from our class are there, too. All smoking.

Elstrom smirks at me.

"The smoking lamp is lit for us, but for Morton, it's the ice cream cone lamp."

Laughter.

"Bite me."

I lick my ice cream at him.

He blows smoke at me.

A car rolls up. Red flag with two white stars on it. The back door opens. General Hockmuth steps out. Starts toward the PX. His likely course goes through the middle of our group.

"Ten-hut!"

What do I do with an ice cream cone in my hand? Salute? Maybe he won't notice the cone if I hold it down at my side.

That's what I do. Cone at my side, I snap out a salute.

"Good afternoon, General."

Returning my salute, he looks down at the cone.

"Good afternoon, Lance Corporal. As you were, before that thing melts."

"Aye-Aye, Sir."

"Coming up in the Corps," a hint of a thin smile, a look of recognition, "Lance Corporal Morton?"

The guys look startled.

"Yes, Sir."

"Congratulations."

"Thank you, Sir."

The guys look back and forth at each other.

"Are you stationed here?"

"Radio Telegraph Operator School, Sir."

The General's demeanor personifies that of a favorite uncle. I like him.

"Good luck, Lance Corporal."

"Thank you, Sir."

Salutes exchange. Into the PX he goes.

Lap up my melting ice cream.

"Holy shit! You know him?"

I nod.

We start back to class. I take bites out of the ice cream.

"He knows you?"

I nod and stuff the cone into my mouth.

"You're lying."

Mouth full of cone, I shrug my shoulders.

"How'd you meet?"

They push hard for answers.

"Come on, Morton."

"It's not much of a story. We met during Mess and Maintenance Week, here in boot camp. That's all."

Let 'em wonder.

The End

"READY?" I ASK, holding open the car door.

"Yes." Karen flashes that big, beautiful smile. The money her folks spent on her teeth was worth it, well spent. Her perfect smile makes her all the more beautiful.

She steps in. Slides to the middle.

I close the door. I'm the luckiest guy in the world.

Around the back of the car. Then, into the driver's seat. We are off for the mandatory counseling with a Navy Chaplain. That's the Marine Corps Way.

If the Marine Corps had wanted you to have a wife, it would have issued you one.

Issue, my ass. Marital counseling? Bullshit.

Drive through the main gate of MCRD, park the car. Hand in hand, we stroll to the Chaplain's office.

At the door, "Wait." Karen loops her arm under and around my arm. Pulls herself close to me, stares at the ground, "I love you, but I can't marry you."

Slammed me in the gut. I don't know what to say. Finally, with as much courage as I can muster, I ask, "If you love me, why not?"

"My parents." She looks back up to me. Tears well up.

"What about them?" My foggy brain realizes what is happening. *Her damn parents.*

"They said they'd disown me if I married you. They wouldn't see me or talk to me ever again."

The entire universe collapses around me. Crushes the air from my lungs. It is just Karen and me in a vacuum.

She cries hard. "I'm so sorry, Tom-Tom." Takes off the ring. Tries to hand it to me.

"No, you keep it." It looks blurry. Can't focus. Push her hand away.

"I can't." She places it in my hand, closes it around the ring. A kiss, "Please. Just take me home."

"Okay. Just a sec." I drop the ring into my pocket.

Knees wobble, legs like logs, I plod to the Chaplain's door, open it, stick my head inside. "Sorry, Padre. Change of heart." I blink my eyes to clear them.

He looks up from his desk.

"Sorry, son. I'll be here if you want to talk about it."

"Yes, Sir."

I close the door, softly.

I return to her. She gazes at me, her golden brown eyes full of tears. They feed the twin streams that spill down her face. Lowers her head, looks down. Her tears drip onto the ground.

Now what? What do I say? What do I do?

My eyes sting.

Do what she asks. Take her home, I guess.

Legs stronger, I step closer, cup her face in my hands, tilt it up to mine. Kiss her.

"It's okay." *Not really.* "I understand." *Bullshit.*

She pulls me to her with one of her squeeze-her-love-into-me hugs.

Eyes close. Absorb all her love. I know this is the last time.

A somber, quiet drive to her house. She cuddles next to me, head on my shoulder. Her occasional sniffles stab my heart.

No reaction from me. I am stoic, numb.

The drive drags on and on. I do not want it to end. But, I know it is over.

I park in my usual spot, turn off the car, start to open my door. Her hand touches my elbow.

"No. Stay here."

I turn to her. She cups my face in her hands. One last kiss.

I will always remember your soft lips, soft kisses, tender love.

She slides out the passenger door, gently shuts it, turns, walks out of my life. I watch her all the way to the door. Just before I look away, she turns to me, lowers her head, turns back away from me, opens the door, and is gone.

Goodbye, Karen. I will always love you.

Hands together on the steering wheel, I put my head on them. A few seconds pass.

Raise my head.

Stare out the windshield.

Start the car.

Drive off.

The steering wheel is wet.

Let's Party

GOTTA DO SOMETHING today. Call a frat brother. Maybe something's happening.

"Hi, Greg.

"Yeah, it's me.

"Nope. Not in Viet Nam. Yet.

"I don't want to talk about her. Just touching bases. See what's going on.

"Today?

"Eleven o'clock at El Monte Park. Got it.

"Fucking-A-Tooty, I'll be there!

"Another one in Santa Ana? Afterwards? Are you shitting me?

"Yeah, yeah. I know you wouldn't do that. I'm your favorite turd. Hardy har-har.

"Absolutely I'll be there.

"Outstanding. Later."

Noise from the party beckons. Rocks out. Drinking to the max. Nonstop dancing. A blast in mid explosion.

And it is pledge week. I have wanna be brothers to put through my improvised boot camp. Pledges, the boots of fraternities. The brothers, the drill instructors.

A bottle of 12 year old Scotch liberated from my stepfather's liquor cabinet in hand, I march five pledges out to a field, away from the party.

They struggle through jumping jacks, sit-ups, squat thrusts, push-ups, duck walks. *I did 'em. You can do 'em.*

Through the lips, over the gums, look out stomach here it comes. A swig of Scotch flows down, coats my throat with warmth. Suck in a deep breath. Every bit of my innards flames up as the golden liquid makes its way to my stomach.

Ahhh! No shit, look out stomach.

"Guards up!" Comes from the main party area. Phi Sigma's call to a fight.

Off to the ruckus. Over my shoulder, I bark, "Follow me."

Without hesitation, they do. The brawl is in full swing. Somebody grabs me from behind. I turn. My fist hammers into the guy's face. Knocked off his feet, he splats onto the ground. Blood gushes from his nostrils, seeps out his mouth. Out cold.

Welcome to the twilight zone, asshole. Courtesy, USMC.

Sirens blare in the distance.

Time to split.

Everyone scatters, scrambles into cars, cuts out.

Back at the frat house, we load up. Head north to Santa Ana.

This party rocks out. The usual. Drinking, dancing, rowdiness.

I wake up in the middle of the dance floor, on my stomach, a pillow under my head. I roll over.

Eye-burning sunlight streaks in from a lone window. Slams my eyelids shut. Ease them open. Scope out the room. A pledge, in a corner, looks like a curled up pill bug.

My head feels like a bowling ball as I crawl over to him.

"Rossi." Shake him awake.

My stomach does a flip-flop. A dry heave. *Peachy.*

Another dry heave. Deep breath pants calm things down.

"Rossi. You okay?"

"Sir, yes, Sir."

I am not convinced. He looks as awful as I feel.

We help each other up. Lean against a wall for a few seconds.

"Let's take a look around."

"Sir, yes, Sir."

Mason, another pledge, sits on the floor, propped up against a beer keg. A few shakes of his shoulder does not roust him from his stupor. Pulling his legs until his head hits the floor, does. His eyes look like an angry bull's, ready to charge. He backs off when he realizes who awakens him. "Sir?"

"You're damn right, Sir."

"Sir, sorry, Sir."

We find three more brothers. They look terrible, too.

"Let's get some breakfast. Go home."

"I need a ride." Gibson belches.

"Me, too."

"You guys seen Higgins?" Williams looks around at our little group, all shaking our heads.

"Great. I rode up with him. I need a ride back."

"Anyone got a car?"

"Yeah. I got mine." Carson, the only affirmative answer.

Swell. Six of us in a Ford Falcon.

"Good, Carson. You're driving."

"Duh."

"Shotgun!"

"Pledges don't get shotgun. Shotgun." Williams wastes no time yelling out. Amble out to Carson's car, no one falls down.

We jostle our way into the car. Doors close. Someone farts. Windows roll down. In a hurry. In a panic. Too slow. Too late.

"Who the hell shit his pants?"

Carson eases out into the sparse Sunday morning traffic. "Well? Do we eat?"

No answer.

"Split for home?"

"Eat."

"Yeah."

"I don't know."

Me, either. I wrap arms around stomach, hold it in tight.

Grunts and groans sum up the answers as yeses.

"Up there, on the right. An IHOP."

Carson aims his car into the parking lot. Does a decent parking job. Almost.

"I don't know about this."

Grunts and groans. We tumble out of the car. Drag ourselves into the restaurant.

"Good Morning." The hostess escorts us to a table big enough to give us each some elbow room. She shuffles menus to us. She is way too cheery.

"Anything to drink?"

In unison, "Coffee!" *The Mormon Tabernacle Choir.*

"Coming right up. Jennifer, your waitress, will be with you shortly."

A busboy brings the coffee.

A sip. Burns my lips and tongue. I don't care. *Aaaaah, that's better.*

Big breakfasts all around.

"Morton, you were absolutely ape-shit last night."

Mouth full of pancakes, I scan the table. All eyes on me. All indicate agreement.

"What?"

"You leaped from the second floor balcony onto the roof of the church next door."

"Bullshit."

"No, really."

"Bullshit."

"Swear to God. And you climbed up onto the cross up on the front of the church."

Still in agreement as they shovel pancakes, eggs, sausage, ham, and bacon into their mouths. And wash it down with coffee.

"You was singing that Marine song."

Marine Corps Hymn, you idiot.

"Bullshit."

"No bullshit, brother. A bunch of us went outside to the front of the church. We tried to coax you down. You wouldn't budge."

"You kept swinging around on it."

"And up and down."

"A tail and you'd look like a monkey."

"Bullshit."

"No kidding, man. It took us forever to pull you down." *Jesus.*

Heads nod. Shoveling the chow continues.

"We finally got you back to the party."

"You found a bottle of booze. And went to slugging it down while dancing. With no one." *Oh, man.*

I try to not look sheepish. I am unsuccessful, I'm sure.

Snickers and snorts pepper my ears. *Real fucking funny.*

"Then, you crashed."

"But, you didn't burn."

"I woke up with a pillow under my head."

"Sir, I lifted your head up and slid it under you, Sir."

"Thanks, Mason."

Breakfast over, we pay. Start to the car. One by one, we get sick, rush to the curb, and start barfing. Here we are, next to an IHOP, blowing chunks of our breakfasts into the gutter as the Sunday morning church crowd pulls into the parking lot.

It's us, people, not the food.

Breakfast expelled, we cram into Carson's Falcon. He sets course for home.

Even with the windows down, not enough air blows through to remove the stink of booze, beer, barf, farts, and stale smoke.

It's gonna be a long ride home.

Lighting Up

SMOKING IS IMPORTANT. I might lose a hand or arm in Viet Nam. I teach myself to light a cigarette with one hand. I practice and practice.

No problem getting a cigarette out of the pack, soft or hard. Place cigarette in mouth.

Dig out Zippo from pocket. Maneuver it in hand so open edge of lighter is at the joint of where the thumb joins the hand. Closed edge sits at first knuckle of index finger. Sharply flick hand down and away, stop quickly. Zippo pops open. Spin ignition wheel with thumb, flame up.

Light cigarette.

Put out flame by snapping lighter shut with reverse motion that opened it. Return lighter to pocket.

Enjoy.

A book of matches is tougher.

Hold book of matches with back of book against index and middle fingers. Slide flap of book open with thumb. Curl a match out of the book, keep it attached, in one piece curved in an arc, head of match resting on striking surface. Close match book.

Press thumb on match head and slide on striking surface.

Remove thumb from match head before flame bursts out.

Light cigarette. Extinguish match. Take a drag and enjoy.

Oh hell, just carry strike anywhere matches.

Diane

"GOING OUT WITH her again tonight?"

"Yes, Mom. And, her name is Diane, Mom."

"Just because she called to see how you're doing doesn't mean you have to take her out every night for what, a month? Two months?"

"I don't know. Who cares? Are you keeping a log or something?"

"Don't get smart with me, young man."

"Yes, ma'am. Sorry."

"It's just that I worry that you're not over Karen, and this one might take advantage."

Again with Karen? Give it up, for crying out loud. I sure as hell have.

"It's okay, Mom."

"She's not a girl like you went steady with when you started high school. She's more of a woman now."

"Yes. I know. And, now I'm more of a man."

"I don't like where this looks like it's going."

"Don't worry, Mom. It'll be okay. Gotta go."

A kiss on the cheek and a hug.

Off to pick up Diane. A movie, then we go to the submarine races.

Tonight's submarine race program is not going well. Only get to the starting gate.

"Come on, honey. We steamed up the windows. No one can see in."

"I don't care. I'm not getting in the back." *We'll see.*

"Why not?"

"I'm saving myself for when I get married." *Ah, jeez.*
"Ok. How about we get married?" *Did I just say that?*
"Do you love me?" She sounds hopeful.
"Yeah. Sure. I guess I do." *Yeah? What the hell?*
"Then, yes. I'll marry you. I love you."
Maybe I should say it. "I love you, too." *Do I? Does it matter?*
See, Karen, someone will marry me. That'll show you.

Orders

RADIO SCHOOL ENDS. I graduate. I am a Radio Telegraph Operator.

My class awaits orders. Most want WESTPAC.

We field day our barracks. When we pass inspection, liberty cards will be issued.

Shepersky, late as usual, stands in the hatch. "Orders just posted on the bulletin board."

A stampede ensues.

Who's going where? Where am I going? Questions on all minds.

A few receive orders to Cherry Point, North Carolina; Camp Lejeune, North Carolina; Camp Pendleton, California; Hawaii.

The rest, WESTPAC. Some to Okinawa. Most to Viet Nam.

Guys want to phone home. Tell their families. The pay phones are in the E-Club. As I am the senior man in our barracks, they ask me for permission to stop the field day long enough to make their calls.

"Sure. Go. Make it quick."

They bolt to the E-Club. I follow close behind.

The guys make their calls.

"Morton!" The Assistant Duty NCO.

"What?"

"Get your people back to the barracks. On the double."

"Orders posted. We're all calling home with the news."

"Corporal Owens says to get back now."

"Fuck off." I walk away to the phone bank.

"Hurry up, guys. We gotta get back now."

Back to the barracks, finish the field day, pass inspection, go to the Duty NCO's desk to sign out my liberty card.

"You're in trouble, Morton." Corporal Owens snarls at me.

"Okay." *No skin off my ass.*

The next day I am ordered to report to the Regiment Commanding Officer, Colonel Jacobs.

I present myself to the Sergeant Major. He stands behind his desk. No smile. His eyes look hard, tough, unforgiving. Cold.

He marches me into the Colonel's office, to the front of his desk. The Colonel sits on the other side. The Battalion Commander, Major Nightengale, stands behind the Colonel, to the right. The Major smiles, slightly. *What's so funny?*

I remain at attention, staring past the Silver Eagles on the Colonel's collar to a portrait of President Johnson on the wall behind the Colonel. *Full Bird.*

"Report!" Bellows the Sergeant Major.

"Lance Corporal Morton reporting as ordered, Sir!"

The Colonel stares at me for a second, then looks at some papers on his desk.

"It says here you said fuck off to the Assistant Duty NCO. Is this true?"

"Yes, Sir." A hard swallow.

He nods, scans my file. Looks up at me.

"What do you have to say for yourself?"

I explain the circumstances.

Lips pursed, he nods several more times.

"Saying that to the Assistant Duty NCO is the same as saying it to the Duty NCO and to the Major here and to me. Did you intend to say that to them, to me?"

"No, Sir!"

"I didn't think so." He thumbs through my file again. "You have a fine record here, Lance Corporal. I hate to see it tarnished."

"Yes, Sir." *But?*

"You are reduced in rank to Private and forfeiture of one month's pay." *Damn.*

"Yes, Sir."

"Suspended thirty days. Keep your nose clean for the next thirty days, you keep your rank and pay. Understand?"

"Yes, Sir."

The Major's smile disappears.

"But, Sir, this man goes on thirty days leave next week."

"I see." The Colonel looks up, smiles, "I guess I gave you a bigger break than I thought. Get out of here!"

"Aye-Aye, Sir!" *Holy shit, that was close.*

The Sergeant Major marches me out. In his office, "You're one lucky son of a gun." He smiles, his eyes now kind. "Enjoy your leave and good luck in Viet Nam."

"Thank you, Sergeant Major."

About face. Then, at flank speed, I leave.

That is how the chain of command works.

To Viet Nam

7 July

THEY HERD US onto cattle cars for transport to the foot of Broadway in San Diego, California. The USNS General John Pope awaits dockside, ready to take us to Viet Nam.

Dad, my stepmother, and Diane are here to see me off. Small talk fills the time before going aboard.

Diane, does not say much. "I'll miss you. Be careful."

"I'll be fine. Nothing's going to happen to me. I think I'll be in a rear area. Most likely away from any action. The kind of radioman I am usually doesn't snoop and poop out in the bush with the infantry."

"Snoop and poop?"

"Snooping is looking for the bad guys. Pooping is what happens when you find them."

She smiles. *Doesn't get it.* Her smile wanes. *Maybe she does.*

My stepmother doesn't say much either. She never does.

Dad says the most.

"Sure you're still going to Viet Nam?"

"Yes, Dad, I'm sure. We aren't going to the Middle East. That war is over."

"Didn't you think you might go there?"

"Yes. Nobody wanted to. Every morning we checked out the headlines. Reaction was Go, Jews. Go. And they did. So now it's off across the big blue pond to our war."

"When you get aboard ship, be sure to get a top bunk. That way, nobody will step on you as they get in and out of their bunks. And no one can puke on you."

"Thanks."

"The first morning, breakfast will be green scrambled eggs. It's only green food coloring. The cooks just like to mess with Marines, make them sick. If you want the chow line to move fast, start gagging like you have dry heaves. This makes the guys in front of you sick and they'll fall out of line to get topside to a rail and puke."

I laugh.

"You laugh, but it's true. This old sailor wouldn't lie to his son. And when you use the head, try to get the stall farthest away from the seaward bulkhead."

"Why?"

"Some smart ass will get in early and get the most inboard stall. He'll wait till the stalls are full. Then, he'll wad up a bunch of newspaper, set it on fire and drop it in the trough."

"So?"

"The trough runs down from inboard to outboard. As the burning newspaper slides down the trough, it singes everyone's butt."

I laugh again.

"While in there, just listen carefully. If you're close enough, you can hear the paper being crumpled. Listen for guys yelling. The flames are loose. Either way, stand up fast."

"Okay, Dad!"

"When you get to Viet Nam, keep your head down. A bullet in the ass is better than a bullet to the head."

"Uh-huh."

Time to board. Hugs and kisses all around. No tears.

Sea bag on my shoulder, I trudge up the gang plank. Wait for a compartment assignment.

I find my way three decks down to my assigned compartment. Maneuver my way around the deck-to-overhead bunks. I muscle my sea bag up onto the first top bunk I find.

Nothing to do now, but wait.

Bored, I go topside to wave goodbye. Family and friends on the dock wave handkerchiefs as the ship sails out of the harbor, off into the sunset.

First stop, Hawaii.

Then, Okinawa.

Finally, Viet Nam.

The first night is uneventful for me. For others, seasickness forces them to the rails topside.

I do not get puked on. *Thank you, Dad.*

Morning is quiet, settled, no one runs topside.

The chow line meanders from the galley, out the passageway and up a stairwell. Too long a wait for me. *Try what Dad said.* "Ugh, ugh, ugh," I gag.

It works.

Guys flee from the chow line, head topside. *Thanks again, Dad.*

Others flee from the galley, not because of me.

Once inside, I see why guys run out. The green eggs look awful. Like something scooped from a stagnant, algae covered pond. *Food coloring. It's only food coloring.*

Next to the green eggs, ham. *Some sailor has a sense of humor.*

Days at sea are full of PT, watching movies, playing cards and acey-deucey, or listening to records played on portable players.

Tournaments keep the troops entertained. Chess, checkers, backgammon, pinochle, and cribbage. The cribbage tournament sounds inviting. I sign-up.

"7."

"15 for two."

"25."

"31 for two."

"15-2, 15-4, 15-6, 15-8, a double-double for 16, makes 24."

"9."

"18, a pair."

"27 for six."

"Go."

"30 for one."

"15-2, 15-4, 15-6, 15-8, 15-10, 15-12, 6 for18 and a pair is 20."

Great cards come my way throughout the enlisted men's tournament. I skunk all my opponents. Because of the great cards, I win the tournament. A match with the officers' champion for the ship championship awaits.

At the appointed time in the officers' lounge, a few decks topside, my opponent, an Army 2nd Lieutenant greets me, a lowly Marine Corps Lance Corporal. The only things make him look older than me are the butter bars on his collar.

Confidence oozes from him. Shyness highlights my demeanor.

He chatters to no end.

Not here for conversation.

I kick his butt. Two skunks.

"Can't you take it easy on me?"

"I just play the cards I'm dealt, Sir."

The butt kicking continues. Win number three activates angst. He squirms in his chair.

"You sure are lucky."

"Yes, Sir." *And I play better that you.*

"This is almost disrespectful. I might file charges." A wry smile.

"Yes, Sir. Your deal, Sir."

"6."

"12 a pair, Sir."

"18 for six." He chuckles.

"24 for 12, Sir." I dare not chuckle.

"Damn!" He is not chuckling.

"Sorry, Sir. Again, it's the cards, Sir."

"31 for two," slaps down a seven. He moves his peg two holes.

He counts first.

"15-2, and a double for 8 gives me 10." He looks up at me. Smiles. *Confident are we?*

He is six from a win. Possible to peg out, too. Doesn't.

I have first count. *He ain't gonna like this.*

"15-2, 15-4, 15-6, 15-8, a double-double for 16 makes 24, Sir. And I'm out. Good playing you, Sir."

Fourth straight win. Butt kicking complete. I win the best of seven match. The ship cribbage championship belongs to me. Big deal. I beat a whiny Army wimp, an officer to boot.

Showers onboard ship are not time consuming. Turn water on, get wet, turn water off, lather up, turn water on, rinse off, turn water off, exit shower. More than five minutes, those in line become rowdy.

21 July

THE POPE DOCKS at White Beach, Okinawa. Elements of the 3rd Marine Regiment disembark. The rest of us are granted four hours shore liberty with a flying 20. Four hours on the white sands of White Beach, next to the dock.

The facilities expect us. Barbecues fired up, cooks cook, waitresses wait to wait, cases of beer on ice. Many, many cases.

My flying 20 signed for and pocketed, I turn toward the stern, salute the flag. Then, hurry down the gang plank. On land, my sea legs feel funny, wobbly. No matter. Full steam ahead to the E-Club. It is packed. Ten minutes pass before I find a seat. I gobble up a steak, with French fries and milk.

Next, some ice cold beer.

I watch guys carry off cases of beer. Not six-packs. Not individual cans. Cases, just one per man.

On my way up to the front of the line I recognize only one brand. Carling Black Label.

"Six-pack of Carling Black Label."

"You have to buy a case."

What the hell. "A case it is."

I squish my way through the sand to join some pals. Open my case, take out a beer, pop it open, then down the ice cold bubbly refreshment. A big beer-steak-fries-milk belch follows. *Ahh.*

Twenty-three beers later, it's back to the ship. As I shuffle through the sand, I think about where the ship takes me and what awaits there. I don't know.

Hoots and hollers jar me back to now. Guys jump off the bow into the harbor. *Looks like fun.*

Go up the gang plank, salute the flag, request and get permission to come aboard, stumble to my compartment.

At the entryway, three black guys jump me. Racial tensions put everyone on edge. I become combative. They subdue me.

"Whoa, Mort! It's us."

I look around. Jenkins, Morris, and Bascom, three of my buddies. I relax. They release me, then rub something on me that's cold, sticky.

"We're smearing ice cream on everybody. Making sundaes. See? We're chocolate sundaes!"

Vanilla ice cream covers their heads and faces. A lick of my lips tells me chocolate coats me.

"You're a vanilla sundae!"

We laugh. *Jeez.*

I go into the compartment to clean up with a shower. At my bunk, I retrieve my record player from my sea bag. Thumb through my albums. Beach Boys, Dylan, Beatles, Stones, Joplin. Indecision wears me out. I crash.

The ship arrives outside Da Nang Harbor at night. We bunch up along the rail.

Big guns fire in the distance. Boom. Boom. Boom.

Occasional flashes of light splotch the horizon. The sea air smells dirty. Sweaty. Scary.

A combat zone. Somewhere Marines fight and die, kill or be killed.

29 July

The ship docks in Da Nang Harbor. The bustle of the landing area kicks up dirt. The air smells and tastes musty. A hot breeze blows the dust through the air. With it comes an odor of dirt, sweat, and cordite. Dry, acrid smells, dusty, dirty. What is that other smell? I don't recognize it.

The smell of war?

Next stop is 3rd MARDIV, HQ BN, Comm. Co., Radio Platoon, someplace called Phu Bai.

First Six Months

Phu Bai

"Dismissed."

Great. Another stupid ass inspection and no one passes.

Cain strides up next to me as we return to our hooch.

"Nice, huh, Morty?"

"You're out of your ever-loving gourd. I tell you. They're crazy! Bat shit crazy!" My arms wave in the air like wings. One wing holds my M16. "No one will ever pass inspection in this dusty red powder crap!"

"No one has since I been here. Except right after monsoon season."

"And, why would that be?"

"This powder becomes sticky, cling-to-everything red mud."

"You pass inspections, then? In that goo?"

"Nope. But, when the rains quit, there's a short time when the mud dries, but isn't dry enough to be this red powder shit." He stomps a foot down. Cloud of red dust billows up.

At the hooch, we lumber over to our cots, dust off our pieces and secure them. Prepare for the rest of the day.

The routine of Third Marine Division, Headquarters Battalion, Communications Company, Radio Platoon, grows old.

Every morning, we stand rifle and personnel inspection. No one ever has a clean rifle or boots. The ground is fine red powder. No matter how hard we try, this fine red powder permeates everything, especially our rifles and boots.

This no win, no benefit, no good routine bores and tires me.

0800

Walgast and me, shirtless and sweating, at the T-site fill sandbags. Place them around the transmitter to prevent damage from enemy fire.

A cool down at noon chow follows the hot morning. After lunch, we go back to the T-site. Fill and place more sandbags. Heat increases. More sweat.

1600

Relief from the tedious work. I go to my hooch, strip down, gather my toiletries, and drag myself to the showers. This time of the year, it is a cold water shower.

Air dry on the walk back to my hooch. Dress for evening chow.

Free time follows. Drink beer or soda, pitch horseshoes, play volleyball, throw a baseball around, write home, or lay around reading letters, books, magazines, or listen to music. The evening brings the day's movie. "What's Up Tiger Lily?" A Japanese spy-thriller dubbed in English with a plot about the world's greatest egg-salad recipe that has been stolen. It's everyone's favorite. Hilarious.

Taps at 2300.

Reveille at 0500. It starts again, the same boring routine.

The only exciting thing that happens since I get here is a rocket attack. We climb up onto the roofs of our hooches or race out onto the platoon street to watch. The rounds land on the parade ground and sports field. The exploding rockets move closer. One bursts at the edge of the field near our hooches. Guys on the roof slide down into the open-pit bunkers next to the hooches, others scurry from the platoon street.

When the attack ends, we wander around giggling, grins on our faces. No one is hurt and no damages. It was close. Not too close, but close enough.

Despite that rocket attack, I remain bored.

A new day and we fill sandbags. A jeep pulls up. Three officers hop out. They walk toward us.

"Ten-hut!" Walgast calls us to attention.

These officers wear clean, crisp utilities. Two are Colonels. The other sports two stars on his collar, a Major General. Not just any Major General, but Major General Hockmuth, my old buddy from MCRD.

"At ease."

They stride around the site, look over our work.

The General asks, "How's it going?"

"Fine, Sir."

"Good, Sir."

He nods. The officer threesome starts back to the Jeep.

The General stops, turns, and walks up to me. I come to attention.

"At ease. Morton, isn't it?"

"Yes, Sir."

I can't help the smile on my face.

"I thought you looked familiar. How long have you been here?"

"A month, Sir."

"How do you like it here?"

"It's okay, Sir." *Boring.*

"I see. Well, good luck and carry on."

"Thank you, Sir."

He joins the other two at the jeep. A cloud of red powder kicks up. Result of their quick departure.

We resume filling sandbags.

A notice on the platoon bulletin board gets my attention. Volunteers are needed for door gunners and CAC.

Door gunner? Man an M60 machine gun on a helicopter? I can do that. CAC? What the hell is that? I don't care. Either one must be better than what I'm doing here.

I volunteer for both.

First Visit

INTO THE FIELD tent. Look for my best man at Diane and my wedding.

Hope this is the right place.

Eyes adjust to the soft light and see a guy sitting on his cot, writing. *Maybe he knows.*

"Is this Recon?"

"That's what the sign outside says."

Friendly s.o.b. "Yeah. Just wanted to make sure. You got a Barnhart here?"

"Yup. Dutch is around here somewhere." Scans the tent.

From somewhere behind me, "Hey, Super Skate."

I spin around. There he is.

"Hey, yourself, Secret Squirrel."

Big hug. Pats on backs. Hold each other at arm's length.

He looks like what Santa Claus might look like as a Marine. Short-hair. Clean-shaven. Pale blue eyes sparkle. Just no stomach that shakes like a bowlful of jelly. More like Charles Atlas. His smile accented by a chipped front tooth and puffy Santa cheeks, mouth full of acorns.

"Man, it's really good to see you. So, how's it hanging?"

"Like it always does. I'm good." His face turns serious. "Still married to that gal? What's her name?"

"Diane. And, yes. Why wouldn't I be?"

"Don't know. Surprised, I guess. You was with that other chick for so long."

Karen, good old Karen.

"And then, she dumps you."

"Yeah, well it's her loss. Not mine. No skin off my ass." *Big fat fucking liar.*

He looks right into my heart. "Uh-huh." He understands. "Come on, Tom, let's go get some chow."

"Let's."

I don't want to talk about it.

Hue City

Trips into Hue break up the monotony of Phu Bai. Not exciting, merely a respite from the mundane, dusty 3rd MarDiv HQ.

With supplies for delivery to our radio unit in Hue, Lambert and I hop into a Jeep. The drive into the city reminds me of Dorothy's entry into the Emerald City in Oz.

Its colorful beauty shows no signs of war. People buzz around, on foot, bicycle or motor scooter. They go about their business. Lush greenery lines the streets that run through the city. Hue reminds me of the TV coverage back home of Saigon.

Hue is cleaner. Well-dressed people crowd the streets. The women wear the Vietnamese traditional national attire, áo dài and conical Vietnamese hat, nón lá. A few Vietnamese soldiers, armed with M1 carbines, roam the streets.

Everywhere are neatly manicured lawns, finely trimmed trees and shrubs, and colorful flowers.

A place of beauty and peace in a country locked in the brutality of an ugly war. Untouched, a place where I and, I'm sure, everyone feels safe.

At the radio site, Rusty offers us cold beers. We accept.

After downing a couple beers, Rusty guides us through the streets to get a close-up look at the ancient Vietnamese Imperial Citadel. Elegant. Magnificent. Breathtaking.

We hurry back to the radio site to get one more beer down the hatch before our return to Phu Bai. Curfew begins at dark. We gulp down that one more beer before sliding into the Jeep.

We speed back to dusty, dirty Phu Bai.

Crap.

CAC

I DON'T GET the door gunner assignment. CAC, Combined Action Company, comes through.

I go to its school, a two week course, in Danang, China Beach. CAC units consist of a squad of Marines and a Corpsman assigned to a village. They work with the village PFs, provide security. Other duties include supplying medical aid, materials for construction of schools and other structures. The goal is to capture the hearts and minds of the villagers.

Instructors teach us basic Vietnamese language, culture, a respect for it and its people.

Additional training includes guerrilla warfare, counter insurgency, ambush techniques, booby-traps, fire team tactics, and basic first aid. Vietnamese chess, xiangqi, turns out to be interesting and fun. It pits two armies against each other. The pieces amuse me. King, Advisor, Elephant, Horse, Chariot, Cannon, and Soldier. Villagers play this game regularly.

Intensive training leaves no time for the war. School runs 0700 to 1600. The rest is free time; no patrols to run, no night ambushes to set up, no guard duty to pull. We spend evenings at the club. Almost like home with cold beer, good food, lively atmosphere, a good band, and friendly bar girls. The band is not American. The club features Vietnamese or Japanese bands. The girls, Vietnamese.

At night, I am most aware of the war. The sounds rumble into my memory. Large guns fire in the distance.

It reminds me of the night before disembarking from the ship in Danang. I think about the same things. Marines killing or being killed. Only difference now, the chatter of small arms fire and the muffled explosions of artillery shells are louder, closer.

No one dies in war. They are killed.

The beat of the band pounds me back to now. Pour another beer down my gullet.

Maybe what I do in CAC will help bring the war to an end.

An added bonus of this school is the location. On a beach. I never thought I would surf in Viet Nam. Yet, here, I am, floating on a 9'10" surfboard, checked out from the China Beach Special Services. I wait outside the break, look out to sea in search of a good wave. One starts to form that looks promising, worthy of my skills. I spin around toward the shore and paddle hard. I catch the nice little five footer.

For a few moments, I am home. Race up and down the face of this wave, the sea spray splashing over and around me. The freedom I feel exhilarates me. Cut back through the wave, turn, paddle back out to catch another one. Need to do it again. I do. Over and over.

The ocean seems the same as back home.

A sea snake swims nearby. La Jolla Shores doesn't have sea snakes.

I am not home. I am in Viet Nam.

Back to reality.

Shit.

Dong Ha

THE END OF CAC training brings the war back to the forefront. Orders to report to CAC-P via air-transport to Dong Ha, somewhere near the DMZ. On the short walk to the C-123, rain from the dark gray sky soaks me and my duffle bag.

The propellers rotate so slow, they seem to stand still. The low rumble of the engines does not sound powerful. *Can this thing even fly?*

I scurry up the rear ramp into the cargo hold. Eyes adjust to the dark. Drag myself to the front, behind the cockpit. Throw my gear up against the bulkhead, under a canvas seat. The crew chief motions me to buckle up. I do. He gives me a thumbs up.

Dong Ha? CAC-P? North. Close to the DMZ. How close? Never mind. For now, a nap.

Head rests back on the bulkhead, eyes close. Engines ramp up to a roar. *Can't sleep. Try.*

The plane lurches forward. Bounces down the runway. Creaks. Nose lifts, pushes me against my seatbelt, toward the rear of the plane. *That was quick.*

The crew chief, belted in on the opposite side of the plane, grins. I must look startled.

Asshole.

The roar of the engines quiets down to a hum. I drift off.

A tap on my shoulder awakens me. I open one eye. It is the crew chief.

"Wake up, sweet pea. We're about to touch down. The air strip is being hit. Rockets and mortars."

Not bored now.

"I throw your duffle bag out, you follow. Find a bunker. Be quick. Good luck."

He grins.

This is funny?

Thumbs up. Him first. Then, me.

The gradual descent turns into a steep drop. An abrupt, loud thud, a couple bounces. The C-123 shudders to a bumpy roll down the runway.

I unbuckle, reel to the ramp. It is open, nearly drags on the runway.

Explosions behind us get my attention. *Not close. Good.*

The plane slows down to a crawl. Explosions continue to follow. Shock waves intensify.

Damn. They're getting closer. Gotta get off this thing.

Duffle bag tumbles down the ramp after a heave-ho from the crew chief. I run down the ramp. Jump. Rain pin-pricks my face. I splash down.

The engines ratchet up to a roar, then fade away.

Explosions get louder. Concussions intensify. The rockets continue their march toward me. *Shit. Move, move, move.*

Scramble up to a crouch. Grab my bag. Break for the bunkers.

"Over here." A hand motions above a face peering out from the sandbag hatch. The hand and face disappear into the inner sanctum of the bunker.

I slosh through the mud. Slide into the bunker. *Safe at home!*

From the darkness, "Welcome to Dong Ha."

First Ambush

MY FIRST NIGHT and I go out on an ambush. I am the new guy. And because I am a radioman, the radio sits on my back. I still wear stateside utilities, no jungle garb yet. Regular issue boots, no jungle boots.

The cool night air brushes across my face. I squish through the wet, slippery ground. Dew drops drip from the vegetation. Dampens me as we make our way to the ambush site. A typical Southeast Asia fall night.

At the ambush site the squad leader whispers, "Sit here. Shoot anything that moves in front of you." He disappears.

With complete trust in my squad mates, I sit; radio on my back, handset clipped to my left shoulder, M16 with chambered round, safety off, butt under my right armpit, right index finger on the trigger guard. Ready for action.

For the longest time, I do not move. Nothing moves. Trigger finger tires. *Stay alert. Be ready.*

The earpiece of my handset crackles, "Tiger Papa Five Alpha. Tiger Papa Five Alpha. This is Tiger Papa Five. This is Tiger Papa Five. Sit rep, over."

What the hell is that? Wasn't covered in Radio School. I don't answer.

"Tiger Papa Five Alpha. Tiger Papa Five Alpha. This is Tiger Papa Five. This is Tiger Papa Five. Sit rep, over."

Perhaps I should say something. In a whisper, "Tiger Papa Five. This is Tiger Papa Five Alpha. Over."

"Five Alpha. This is Five. Sit rep is short for situation report. If all is well, key the handset twice. Over."

Oh, situation report. Sit rep.

As far as I know everything is well, except I don't know where any one is. I key the handset twice.

"Roger. Out."

The ambush lasts four hours. Three more sit reps are requested. Three more times I key the handset twice, still not knowing where any one is.

Sometime after the fourth sit rep, a hand gently grabs my shoulder. My squad leader's voice, "Time to head back. Let's go."

That's an ambush? Nothing moved in front of me. I saw nothing. Nothing happened. Nothing.

Stateside boots cause me to slip and slide on the wet terrain on the way back to the compound.

In the tent, at my cot, I pull off my damp clothes. Sergeant Clark, NCOIC, and my squad leader, Corporal Bulow, approach me. They explain that the radioman stays with the team leader at all times.

"Then, where the hell were you?" I am pissed.

"We left you alone in the Village Chief's yard where we could see you, but you couldn't see us. It was a test to see what you'd do. You done good. You stayed still and quiet, you handled the radio good. Welcome to Papa 5. Your next ambush will be the real deal. You'll be okay when the shit hits the fan."

"Thanks a whole fucking lot."

They laugh and go to their cots.

Not funny, fuckers.

The 'Stache Stays

The Captain holds a rifle and personnel inspection before doling out the dollars.

God, cannot get away from these damn inspections.

When he gets to me, "Shave off the mustache." That's all he says, doesn't look at my rifle.

"Aye-Aye, Sir." *No way.*

He moves to the next guy.

Thirty days later, at the next payday and inspection, the Captain has a mustache, too. His is not as full as mine.

"I thought I told you to shave that mustache off."

"I did, Sir. It grew back."

"Shave it off."

"Sir, according to regulations, NCO's are allowed mustaches as long as they are neatly trimmed. I believe mine is neatly trimmed, Sir."

He starts to say something, but stops. Moves to the next guy.

The 'stache stays until I say so.

First VC

THE DAY LONG drizzle soaks everything it touches. We hear an explosion in the ville, a grenade. We saddle up and rush to the site.

We get to the scene in time to see a lone VC hobbling to escape. He turns to fire at us. We drop him in a hail of M16 automatic fire. His body shimmies from the impact of the bullets, blood bursts into the air. A crazy, angry hive of blood.

Two PFs tie rifle slings around his ankles. They drag him through the village to our compound. His lifeless body slides and slithers along the rain slicked paths. He is like overcooked pasta, his arms long strands of spaghetti. His head bounces like a bobber in water.

At our compound gate, the PFs string him up by all fours on a pole, like a pig over a barbecue pit. We wait for the family to claim his body.

Before they arrive, villagers tell us what happened. The grenade went off, killing the Village Chief. Shrapnel hit the assassin's leg. His wound prevented him from fleeing.

We hear her before we see her. Her wail pierces through the quiet dusk. And through me. I never heard anything like it before now. The grief of a mother who lost a son.

Some villagers cut down her son, carry him away.

She follows behind, her wail, an eerie peal of grief.

I am 19. I learn he was 17.

The blood, his body, her wailing, and our ages stay with me.

The Return

THERE THEY GO. It is a quick month. The platoon supporting the French Fort leaves for Camp Carroll. Then, it is back out to the bush for them.

"Chevy 9 is leaving." Sarge steps up behind me.

"I can see that."

Montanez comes out of the comm bunker, looks around, spots us.

"Hey, Sarge!"

Comes over.

"Chevy 9 just radioed in. They're leaving."

Sarge and I nod toward the rising dust of the departing troops.

"Oh." Montanez returns to the bunker, steps down through the hatch, disappears into its bowels.

"You gonna do your breakfast thing for the new platoon when they get here?"

"Affirmative, Sarge."

"Got enough stuff?"

"All I need is more eggs and bread. We got plenty bacon and coffee."

"Check with HQ."

"Will do." *Might as well do it now.*

It takes a few seconds for my eyes to adjust to the dim light.

"Monty." He looks up from his Dashiell Hammet novel.

"Get a message to Matson."

"Do I need to write it down?"

"Don't think so. Message is, new platoon at the French Fort. Need eggs and bread."

"Got it."

"Good. I'm going to get some sack time. Come get me at noon. I'll take over the radio."

"Okay."

Sarge pokes his head into the mess tent. "Matson's on his way down from the hill. Think he's got the stuff you wanted? It's only been a couple of days."

Finish chewing my mouth-full of spam sandwich, gulp it down, empty my can of Coke. Mouth and throat clear, "We'll find out."

"I guess so." He leaves.

Another soda and the rest of my sandwich in hand, I mosey out to the gate. It takes Matson a few minutes to get down the hill.

The PC stops at the front gate. Matson hops out, goes to the rear of the truck. "Got two flats of eggs. Could only scrounge up eight loaves of bread. Sorry."

"No sweat. They'll be happy with what there is. Thanks."

Supplies unloaded and stored, back to the usual. Nothing. Kill time before patrols during the day and ambushes at night. And, wait for the next platoon to man the Fort.

They look tired, beat up, enough dirt covers them to plant a garden.

New, clean jungles would be nice.

I holler down into the comm bunker, "The new platoon's here, Monty. Come get me when they check in. I'll be in the mess tent."

"All right."

"It'll be a while before they settle in. An hour maybe."

"Okay."

An hour gone, a letter home written, go to the comm bunker to check with Monty.

Should hear soon.

We collide in the bunker's entrance.

"They just checked in."

We step down into the bunker. I lower myself onto the lawn chair facing the radio. Pick up the handset.

"Call sign?"

Monty leans against the wall opposite the radio. "Dragonfly 9."

Handset keyed, "Dragonfly 9. Tiger Papa 5. Over."

"Tiger Papa 5. Dragonfly 9. Over."

"Welcome to our little patch of scenic Southeast Asia. Over."

"Much happening in your little patch? Over."

"Minimal, almost nonexistent. Over."

"Nice. We can use some minimal. Over."

"We have a little tradition for greeting new platoons. A squad at a time comes to our pos. We cook up a regular breakfast, kinda home-style. We can start tomorrow if you can get it cleared with your Six. Over."

"By home-style you mean eggs, bacon, toast, coffee? Over."

"That's affirm. Over."

"Damn. I'm sure Six will okay it. If he doesn't and the guys find out. Never mind. He'll want some, too. Bitchin. Over. Over the white cliffs of Dover."

"Where'd you hear that? Over." *Can't be.*

"What? Over."

"Dover. Over."

"Something I started in radio school. Over." *Son of a bitch. It is him.*

"Daniels?" *Answer, dammit.* "Mike? Over."

"How'd you know? Over."

"Only one dits and dahs s.o.b. I know ever used that. In radio school. Over."

"Morton? Over."

"Yeah. Over."

"I thought I recognized your voice. Didn't think it possible. Over."

"You got some splaining to do. Over."

"Yeah. I s'pose I do. Over."

"Breakfast tomorrow? Over."

"0700? Over."

"Roger. Tiger Papa 5, out."

"Dragonfly 9, out."

Tomorrow should be interesting.

0600

Mama-san arrives at the gate. Goes to our mess tent. After she starts the coffee, I explain some guys from the Fort are coming for breakfast.

She cooks the bacon from the #10 cans as I open them.

0700

They trudge in, led by Daniels. We hug.

"Man, do I have a story to tell you." Shakes his head.

"I'm sure you do. We can talk after breakfast." *Can't wait.*

"Cool."

Before we reach the mess tent, Daniels' buddies start:

"Bacon. I smell bacon."

"Smells fucking wonderful."

"Goddam."

"Uptown."

"Uptown, my ass. Home."

They jabber until I place plates bearing fried eggs on the table.

"Make your own toast on the burner over there. Butter's by the bread."

"Oh, man, butter."

In chow-down mode, their jabber stops. Only grunts, sighs, slurps of coffee, smacks of mouths enjoying good food, the sizzle-crackle of eggs frying, and muffled small talk fill the tent.

0820

As they file out:

"Thanks, man."

"That was awesome."

"Just like home."

"Almost. We're still in the Nam."

Seated across the table from Daniels, a fresh mug of coffee in my hands.

"So, what the hell happened?"

The Story

DANIELS PULLS HIMSELF straight up. Sits erect. Stares down at his coffee, mug in both hands. "I fucked up. Fucked up bad."

"Can't be that bad, Mike. You're here. They give you a Captain's Mast and bust you down to private and take your pay, some confinement?"

"No big deal. Down to PFC plus one month's pay, no brig time or restrictions. Just sent me back to finish radio school."

"That's not so bad. Could've been worse."

"Almost was. It was almost all over."

"How's that?"

"I was in the Tijuana jail for a couple of months."

"What the fuck? You gotta be shitting me."

"Nope. Wish I was. It sucked the big one. Big time."

"Well, no shit."

"Place was dark, damp, hot, sweaty, smelled bad with piss, shit, puke, smoke, sour food. And always some greasy spic trying to beat the shit out of me. It was a goddam battle. Every day."

"I heard it was like that. For us gringos especially. How'd you make it out in one piece?"

"Kept those assholes from getting behind me. Nobody was going to get me from the back. After a couple of days, a few of them took a liking to me."

"How'd that happen?"

"This one that spoke some English said that I was macho, some sort of bad ass. And, that I didn't cause no trouble. I got the feeling that wasn't all."

"Probably wasn't."

"I got the feeling they expected something in return from the rich American."

I chuckle, "Didn't they know you were a low-paid Marine?"

"Marine, yeah. Low pay, no. I was still an American. All Americans are rich."

Takes a sip of his coffee. Holds out his mug. I pour refills for both of us.

"Turns out I was right. They did want something in return."

"What did they want? What did you do?"

My pack of Marlboros out of my pocket, flip the box open, shake a few partially out. Daniels takes one. I pull one out for me.

"I did nothing for what I found out later was a month."

"A month? A whole fucking month?" *Jeez.*

"It took them that long to find me. The Corps and my old man. Mostly my old man."

Flip open my Zippo. Spin the wheel. Whoosh. Instant flame. Light up. Smoke circles around the table between us.

"So. I get a note from a guard." A drag from his cigarette sends more smoke billowing above the table. "It said, Write your name down. Will try to get you out."

His lips press together, eyes water. "It was signed by my dad."

I reach across the table, pat his hand. Chin on his chest, he stares into his coffee, cigarette in his mouth, smoke wafting around the table.

"It's okay, Mike."

A nod, then, "The guard gives me a pencil. I wrote, Cigarettes, Dad."

"That's it? Cigarettes, Dad?"

"I figured he'd get it. The guard took the note and pencil and left."

Shake my head is all I can do.

"A few days later, the guard brings me a package. It'd been opened."

"Of course. Some for them. Some for you."

"Exactly. Anyway, there was three cartons of smokes and some matches. The note said, Five cartons, see you soon."

"The sons of bitches took two cartons."

"At least I had some to share with my," he smiles, "amigos. I instantly had a bunch more of them."

Another chuckle from me. "Natch. American cigarettes."

"Free, too. So, to make a long story short, it took the Corps and my dad and some government people another month to get me out."

"Damn."

"Really. It was pure hell in there. Viet Nam is a walk in the park compared to that fucking hell-hole. Every day was a fight for life. Here, the fight for life is only occasional."

"Man." Swirl my coffee around, take a gulp.

"Uh-huh."

"How the hell did you end up in the TJ slammer, anyway?"

An evil grin emerges. "Well," he laughs. "That night we went to TJ?"

"What about it?"

"I left you guys to explore the bars. Man, there's a ton of dark places. All dives. Lots of whores."

"I know. Been there. Done that."

"Oh, yeah I remember. Since you was 16. So you said."

A grin and a nod from me.

"So's anyways, I'm in this one shit hole when my glass slips from my hand and shatters on the bar."

That's not good.

"I'm pissed. It was almost full. I barely touched it. Then, the bartender comes over. I tell him I'm sorry. He just says twenty dollars. I ask him what for. He points to the broken glass. I tell him no way. He says something about twenty dollars and policia. Now I get real fucking pissed. So, I pick up the bottom of the glass and shove the broken edges into his face and twist it a couple times. You shoulda heard him scream. I figured it was time to boogie. But, before I could get out the door, the policia were coming in. The bartender yelled something. They grabbed me and started beating the hell out of me. Next thing I know, I'm in some god-awful sewer pit."

"The Tijuana jail."

"Affirmative."

"Smooth move, Ex-Lax."

"I know. I know."

The grin returns. Not evil. More mirthful. With pursed lips, "I shan't fucking do that again."

"Good for you, shit-for-brains."

"Yup."

"Yup."

We both laugh, softly.

"How much did it cost your old man to get you out?"

"He wouldn't tell me. Just that the bartender got the most, plus medical. The prick."

"At least you're out, buddy."

Tosses his cigarette into his coffee cup. "I gotta get back." He jolts up to his feet.

My arm around his shoulders, we walk out to the gate.

With a hug, "Thanks, Tom."

"No problem, my man."

He exits, starts up the path to the Fort.

"When you get back to the world, numb nuts, stay out of the Tijuana jail."

Right hand in the air, a little wave, doesn't look back. "Roger that."

Daniels, you're one lucky son of a bitch.

Snipers

A GOOD NIGHT for hunting. The sky is clear, full of stars. Perfect for the snipers assigned to us. The stars provide excellent light for their starlight scope.

The kill zone for our ambush is a small footpath coming out of an area of vegetation. It crosses a creek. Our position is 300 yards away, just below the crest of a hill. In sitting positions to avoid silhouettes, we wait. The snipers settle in to my right. Two PFs face the opposite direction to make sure no bad guys sneak up behind us.

The snipers take turns looking through the scope at the opening in the vegetation. Simmons hands the rifle to me. My look through the scope astonishes me. The scene looks clear as day.

Forever passes. Simmons taps me, hands me the rifle, and points toward our kill zone. I raise the rifle, peer through the scope. Three men come out of the vegetation. I can make out facial features. I hand the rifle back to Simmons. He raises it, sights in, BANG!

The crack of the M14 triggers our ambush. We open up on full automatic. Empty one magazine. Reload. Take the handset from my radioman.

"Five. Five Alpha. Pop illum. Out."

"On the way. Out."

I hear the thumk of our 60 mm mortar fire. In seconds, an illumination round lights up the area. Two bodies visible, one on the path, one in the creek.

The illum round drifts off. The light fades.

"Five. Five alpha. Pop another. Out."

"Roger. Out."

Another thumk. The illum pops above us. I see the feet of a body as it is dragged into the vegetation. We open fire again. It chews up the area. Pieces of green matter burst into the air.

The illum goes out. Simmons scans the area.

"Nothing."

I nod. Rise to my feet. The squad does the same. Driscoll starts off angling down the slope to the right. The squad follows. We edge down 150 yards. We halt, go down on one knee facing the kill zone. Simmons scans the area.

"Nothing." Again.

We sweep toward the zone.

At 75 yards, "Five. Five alpha. Pop another. Out."

"Roger. Out."

Thumk.

We open fire. It rakes the opposite shoreline and the trail into the vegetation.

Our sweep through the area results in no weapons, no bodies, only blood trails and a few scraps of cloth. Charlie made a clean getaway with all weapons, his dead and wounded.

"Five. Five alpha. Be advised no weapons, no bodies. Blood trails and cloth found. One enemy KIA probable and unknown wounded. No return fire. No casualties. Moving on to check point delta. Out."

"Roger. Out."

We start back to the compound, wind through three checkpoints until, "Five. Five alpha. Be advised nearing gate. Over."

"Roger. Come on. Over."

"Roger. Five alpha, out."

"Five, out."

Back inside we talk about the ambush. Simmons says he hit his target clean.

We are a happy bunch. One probable kill, maybe more, and at least one wounded.

No good guys hurt.

It is a good night.

Kit Carson Scout

THE MARINE CORPS embraces the Chieu Hoi program. Chieu Hois are former enemies. The Marine Corps wants Chieu Hois. The Marine Corps dubs them Kit Carson Scouts.

Li Da, our Kit Carson Scout, is a young family man. He tires of being hungry, cold, wet, and on the run. Li has family issues, issues of safety. He fears if found out to be a VC, his family would suffer. He sees his side losing. Li Da Chieu Hois.

The Marine Corps trains and issues him standard Marine gear. We treat Li as one of us. We do not think of him as a gook. The Vietnamese regard him a Marine and treat him as such.

Li lives with us in our field tent. He eats what we eat, not knowing what it might be. He likes the food. When he asks, we tell him what he is eating. We explain what is important or what he might find interesting about the food.

My fire team sits in our tent eating Vienna sausage out of the can. Li asks to try one. I give him one. He likes it. Asks what it is.

I reply, "Duck dicks."

He pales, eyes bug out. Shocked, his mouth flies wide open.

I burst out laughing, so does my fire team. He gets the joke. I tell him what the ingredients are. He prefers that explanation.

Just before Tet, HQ pulls us out of our AO. Li leaves his wife and kids behind, including his newborn son. Upon his return, two weeks later, he finds his wife battered and bruised, tortured by the NVA. They did something to her that stopped her production of milk. She can no longer nurse her baby. Li's family suffered at the hands of the NVA. But they survive. Li's report angers and saddens us. Anger because we aren't there to protect them. Sad because of the brutality they suffer.

During Tet, Li Da proves himself loyal to his Marine brothers. When the RFs run off, he and another Kit Carson Scout hold the north wall of Cam Lo District HQ. They fire the two 30 caliber machine guns the RFs abandon. When they run out of ammo, they revert to grenades and their M16s.

I hear they are awarded Bronze Stars with Combat V.

Li remains with our unit. When I go home in July 1968, I wish I could bring him and his family to America. I don't know what happens to him. I hope he and his family survive, live a peaceful, happy life. They deserve it.

Li Da is my friend.

Doc Leaves a Mark

Doc Young, our Corpsman, holds MEDCAPS once a week. He treats sniffles, colds, flu, sores, open wounds and gashes from farm tools—most require stitches—abscesses that must be drained and compacted with sterilized antibiotic-soaked gauze. He dispenses pain meds, antibiotics, gives injections, as needed. Emergencies as they happen. For security, one of us goes with him. Doc holds his clinics on the outskirts of the ville, on the main road, or in the village square. Long lines greet him each time he holds a MEDCAP. Many walk for miles from outlying areas to attend. Once in a while, Doc makes a house call.

Villagers in the compound after dark are forbidden, except for the PFs and the Village Chief.

A girl, three or four years old, falls into a barbed wire fence, slashes her nose open. Her parents bring her to our compound at nightfall. They want Bac Si Doc to do something. We bring the family into the compound, take them to Doc's tent. The little girl cries uncontrollably. Her parents try to comfort her.

"Let's get her onto the cot." Doc motions to it. The parents set her down.

Doc grabs what he needs from his medical bag. Pulls up a stool. "Hold the light closer."

Baldwin brings the lantern nearer her head.

"Not in my way." Baldwin backs away a bit.

"That's better." Doc stops the bleeding and cleans the wound. "Two or three stitches should do the trick."

He looks at the parents. They cling to each other. The mother looks petrified. The father, more concerned than scared. Doc takes a deep breath, turns to the girl. She thrashes about.

"You look a little nervous." I see it in his face.

"I don't want there to be a scar uglier than absolutely necessary. Hold her head still."

Her head in my hands, she stops crying and calms down to light trembling.

Doc goes to work. Takes his time. Does a great job. The girl's trembling gives way to occasional shakes.

The parents thank Doc as we escort them to the gate. They pass through, fade out onto the path into the darkness.

"Good work, Doc."

"Yeah. We'll see."

Christmas Thanks

Cam Lo, Viet Nam
27 Dec. 1967
Dear Val,

You won't believe what a ruckus you and your friends made with your "care cans."
You should have seen the guys open them. Thanks for sending something for everyone.
We put the Christmas tree up right away. What odd ornaments. Weird shapes.
Where did you find them? I never saw ones like that before. The tree stood tall, even
though it's only 18 inches. We had ducks for Christmas dinner. Weird, huh? Our
supply guy came through the day before Christmas. He had a case of ducks. He said
we could have them if anybody knew how to cook them. Otherwise he was going to give
them to the villagers. All I know about cooking ducks is that you could stuff them
with apples. I had several cans of diced apples in the mess hall. So I had the stuffing.
All that was needed was a little salt and pepper and voila! Ducks for Christmas
dinner. Then we had those great cookies you guys sent. Val, it made this Christmas
a lot better than it could have been. Thank you. They wanted me to make sure to
tell you thank you and your friends, too. A day or two before your stuff got here,
Rivett got a package from his mother. A BIG package of Hiram Walker flavored
brandies. Cherry, peach, and apricot. We took about 3 or 4 days to drink them.
Wanted them to last. These care cans meant more to us than the care packages you,
mom, and grandma sent. The jiffy pop was a big hit. Popcorn in the Nam? Ha!
Ha! I was stingy with the pepperoni. Wasn't hard. Only Baldwin and Harper
wanted any. Of course, grandma's chocolate chip and oatmeal-raisin cookies didn't
last long. Everybody wanted those! Good thing she sent so many! The Kool-Aid was

a big hit, too. Well, little sister, I got to go. Say hi to everyone. Give my love to all. And thank your friends again. Care packages and care cans are always welcome. Hint. Hint.

Love,
Tommy

P.S. Letters are welcome, too.
Me, again.

Second Visit

"DUTCH AIN'T HERE no more. Gone."

"Gone?" My chest forces out a sigh. *Can't be.*

"Not gone—gone. He ain't dead. Shot up pretty bad though. Medevac'd. Can't say what happened after that."

"Any way to contact him? An address?"

"Last we heard he was on the Repose."

"Got his service number?"

"Let me have a look-see."

Have something, dammit.

"Here ya go."

"Thanks."

Been a month. No reply. Just dash another letter off.

Another month. Another mail call. And, still no reply from Dutch. Must not have made it.

"Shit."

Convoy

A CONVOY IS ambushed enroute to Camp Carroll from Cam Lo District Headquarters.

A reaction force rushes out.

They return with a deuce and a half packed with dead Marines wrapped in ponchos. Someone shouts, "One's alive. He moved!"

I throw open a poncho. He is not alive. I throw open several more ponchos. None are alive.

They are ashen gray, drained of blood. Torn apart by small arms, rocket, and mortar fire.

All dead. All Brother Marines. My first dead Marines.

My stomach churns. Nothing comes out. A couple dry heaves.

I am angry.

Angry as hell.

A grieving anger.

1968

Tet

AFTER THREE DAYS of around the clock alert, CAP P-5 pulls out of Dóc Kình. Intelligence reports an attempt to overrun our compound imminent. Support, fire power and troops, are no longer available to us. We are forced to abandon the village we live in, the people we learn to love, the people we protect from the VC as best we can, and the PFs who live with us, run ambushes with us, walk patrols with us, defend our compound and their village with us. Our withdrawal forces them to be on their own, left to the whims and atrocities that could befall them at the hands of the VC and NVA.

We pack up our personal belongings and as much other gear as we can, destroy the rest.

Tanks take us to Camp Carroll.

0100 2 February

After a night of poker in MACV's Mess Hall, I post a volunteer from the added support Marine squad to the comm bunker. He relieves Del Rio on radio watch.

I hit the rack; boots placed on the deck, in the center of my rack, so I can easily slip into them; my steel pot on the ammo crate at the head of my rack, ready to be placed on my gourd with my left hand while slipping into my boots; flak jacket at the foot of my rack, positioned just right to raise onto my right shoulder; my M16 next to my flak jacket to pick up with my left hand. It is then a simple matter to switch my rifle from left hand to right hand and slip my flak jacket to my left shoulder as I race out the hooch to the comm bunker if and when the shit hits the fan, as is expected anytime, any night. As a radioman, I belong in the comm bunker when said shit hits the fan.

I try to catch some sleep before my 0300 turn on radio watch.

The volunteer on radio watch wakes me up.

"I just got a message from Grasshopper 9. I don't understand it."

I look at my watch. *0200.* Slip on my boots. Grab my steel pot, put on my flak jacket, pick up my rifle. "I'll have look."

We steal out the hooch to the bunker.

He shows me the message he jotted down.

Brevity code.

"Grasshopper 9. Tiger Papa. Over."

"Grasshopper. Over."

"Be advised we do not have new brevity code. Use other means or send in clear. Over."

"Wait one."

KABOOM!

Explosions. Gun fire. I peer through the rifle slit of the bunker. The quad 50s ablaze, a lone silhouette on the one on the right, facing east, a dark figure engulfed in bright orange flames. Explosions, fires everywhere. A fuel barrel next to the MACV building explodes. I am back on the radio in less than five seconds.

"Grasshopper 9, Tiger Papa. Be advised, I think I know what you were trying to tell us. Commence on-calls. Over."

"Roger."

"Tiger Papa, off net. Out." I switch to the frequency of the Army artillery unit in Dong Ha. Request their on-calls as well.

Back to my primary net.

"Grasshopper 9, Tiger Papa, switch to illumination. Over."

Halligan comes flying into the bunker, "Shit! Three days to go. Three fuckin' days."

The Major follows him. Looks to me.

"Artillery requested and rogered. Illum requested, no response, Sir."

"Artillery's on target. Well done."

"Grasshopper 9, Tiger Papa. Over."

No response.

"Grasshopper, Tiger Papa, over."

Again, no response.

Antennae must be gone, blown away. I can transmit, but not receive. Change frequency.

"All stations, all stations, this is Tiger Papa. This is Tiger Papa. Switching to alternate frequency. Switching to alternate frequency. Out."

In the darkness, I hold down switch to light the dial while changing to the alternate frequency. To get to the radio on a waist high shelf next to the bulkhead, I bend over to the level of the dial. The Major places his hand on the small of my back, looks over my shoulder.

An explosion is the last thing I remember before I come to, flat on my back, against the opposite wall. The cobwebs begin clearing. The side of my face burns, hot. I get to my feet.

The Major lies on his back beside me. He isn't moving.

I go to the radio, check the frequency. It is correct.

"Grasshopper 9. Tiger Papa. Over."

"Grasshopper 9."

"Illumination?"

"Up."

"Roger."

Return to the Major. One look with my flashlight tells me there isn't anything I can do for him. Many shrapnel wounds to his head and his fixed pupils tell the story. I tend to the wounds of the others. Most are minor, need only pressure bandages to stop the bleeding.

Halligan is another matter.

"Shit! Three fuckin' days!"

He is a mess but conscious. Sits upright, tries to light a cigarette. His face drips blood onto his shirt, forming polka dots. Polka dots of blood.

"Where do you hurt?"

"All over. Three fuckin' days."

I light his cigarette, tear open his shirt. Shrapnel holes stipple his chest.

No sucking chest wound. Good.

No spurting blood, only minor oozing, nothing that needs immediate attention.

"My wrist is fuckin' killing me." He holds up his left arm.

Roll up his sleeve, I see his wrist is broken and bleeds. Not spurting, bleeds none the less. *Stop the bleeding.*

"Hals, this might hurt."

"I don't fuckin' care. Three fuckin' days"

I straighten his wrist as best I can, apply a bandage as tight as I dare. He doesn't flinch. Blood seeps through, then stops.

"My eye fuckin' hurts, can't fuckin' see out of it."

"Which?"

"Left."

Looking into his eye with my flashlight, I see a piece of shrapnel lodged deep in his eye. *Any deeper, you're dead.*

"You'll be okay. Morphine?"

"Fuck no! Three fuckin' days. "

From the moment I come to from being knocked on my ass, till that last Three fuckin' days, all is quiet. Serene. Peaceful. Floating along, doing what I need to do. Tend to the wounded. No urgency. Routine. All under control. The roar of continuous explosions of rockets, mortars, grenades, artillery, pops of illum rounds, the chatter of M16s and AK47s, the rapid thuds of M60s fire become audible again. The rat-a-tat-tat of the RF's and PF's 30 caliber machine guns, M1s, and carbines. The noise brings me back to the battle raging outside. All music to my ears as it means survival. All terrifying as it means death. All confusing.

Captain Macias bursts into the bunker.

"Where's the Major?"

I look toward the Major. He follows my gaze.

"Damn. Adjust: Alpha, right 50. Bravo, down 50. Charlie, left 50. Delta, up 50. Stay in the door way. Protect the radio."

"Aye, Sir."

He returns to the fight.

I radio in the adjustments, find my rifle, crouch in the entrance. Seconds later, the Senior Medic rushes past me, straight to the Major. Starts CPR. I go to him.

"He's gone."

"Yeah. I know. Had to try."

He hangs his head, places his hand on the Major's forehead. Mumbles something, gets up, exits. We all love the Major. We'll mourn later, each in our own way.

At my post, the noise of the battle is much louder, the flashes visible. Nothing near me. I feel safe. For now the bulk of my duty is over, done, complete. All that is required of me is; protect the radio, call in arty adjustments, and keep tabs on the survivors in the bunker.

"Three fuckin' days." *You're doing ok.*

The Captain is back.

"Adjustments 25 each, in."

I turn to the radio.

He stops me dead in my tracks with, "Next adjustment will be onto this position. At my command only. Understand? My command only."

"Aye, Sir."

Again, he is gone.

I understand alright. Means the wire's breached. We're being overrun.

I radio in the adjustments.

The wounded are ok. *They will make it, if…. Even Three Fuckin Days will survive. If….*

Back to my post at the entrance of the bunker.

Outside, day pushes away the night.

Dawn.

I'm still here. We're still here. We are going to make it.

The Captain returns. He half smiles, "Roll 'em out."

"Aye, Sir."

"If anyone, anyone, comes from that area," he points north and northeast of my position, "Shoot 'em."

"Aye-Aye, Sir."

He goes back to wherever he came from. I radio in the adjustments, then return to my post.

Enough light now, I see through the building to the north. Rubble replaces the wall that had been where I stand. It covers the area where the building once stood, totally toppled.

Things start to quiet down. The battle moves away. The sound of chopper blades beats its way into my heart.

The Captain pokes his head through the hatch. "Cease fire. Well done."

"Aye, Sir."

He leaves. I radio in the "Cease fire. Well done."

Back to my post, rifle in hand. At the north end of the demolished building, a lone figure walks over the rubble toward me. I raise my rifle. Sight in. *Identify target.*

"Oliver!" I lower my rifle. "You dumb shit. Why are you over there?"

He smiles, continues past me, toward the MACV HQ building.

Above the fading sounds of a fire fight I hear voices. It's over. I call in to the wounded. We move out into the compound main. A medevac chopper sets down. I go over to help load our dead and wounded onto the chopper. The dead wrapped in ponchos, the wounded on stretchers.

We load the wounded onto the choppers. After we load one of the wound-ed, Hartman asks, "Know who that was?"

"No."

"Doc."

"Young?"

Eyes watering, he nods. The chopper lifts off. I did not recognize Doc Young, our Papa 5 Corpsman, one of my best friends. He looked gaunt, shrunk-en down from his normal hulk of a man. *Dehydration?*

Dust gets in my eyes from the lift off.

All the wounded medevac'd, I help guard the captured NVA soldiers. They are a sorry looking lot. Most wounded, all dazed. One exception doesn't look dazed, a bullet lodged in his lower leg, no blood. He can only hop on his other leg. I help him sit down. He is larger than the rest. *Not NVA. Chinese? An advisor?*

When we load the prisoners onto a deuce and a half, he isn't able to climb aboard. I boost him up. He turns to me as he sits on the edge. Our eyes lock onto each other's. We understand, as stoic as we remain, we understand each other. As if we become friends at this instant.

A few of our men receive Bronze Stars with Combat V. Fewer receive Silver Stars of who I know one, Doc Young. One Navy Cross, to Pinky Hartman, our company clerk. I hear he knocked them dead with his M60. Many Purple Hearts earned. One Medal of Honor awarded to a Marine Corporal, who I think I played poker with before the attack.

As far as I know, Americans killed in our compound number seven and two RFs or PFs. The enemy suffered a few hundred killed. Before their bodies start to rot, filling the air with dead body stench, they are burned up with flame throwers, then bulldozed under.

2 February 1968

I will remember this day. Not so much for what happened, but because it is the end of my dwindling innocence. The day of my closest brush with death, my day of "heroic achievement," my "finest hour."

That's the way it is for me. A good friend lost, an unlikely friend perhaps gained, both never to be seen again. Many killed, a few heroes, most unknown to each other. All giving all for each other. Such is the way of men in battle.

Second Six Months

Message from Home

Pair of jacks, eight, nine, ten. At least I can open. Go for the straight? We'll see.

Simmons puts the deck down. He picks up his cards, squeezes them out in his hand, one at a time. I look around the table. Nothing to see but poker faces.

Simmons puts his cards on the table, turns to Doc. "Well?"

Doc stares at his cards. "Nope."

"Hell, no." Davis closes his hand over his cards.

"I open." Pinky peels a pair of one dollar bills from his stack of money in front of him and tosses them into the pot. "Two bucks."

Davis doesn't wait for his turn. He throws in his cards.

One less to worry about.

"You guys were hit hard, huh?" Davis is not in the game anymore.

"Yeah." Pinky turns to me. "You in or what?"

"Hold on." *Probably has me beat. Jacks or better. Yeah. Has me beat. Maybe out draw him, catch the straight.* "Call." Toss in my two bucks.

"Raise two." Simmons has my attention.

"What happened?" *Shut up, Davis. We're playing poker.*

"They hit us. We hit back, gave 'em hell. We won. They lost."

I don't let Pinky slide by with that. "He's being modest. He kicked ass with the 60. Even changed the barrel once. Kept mowing them down."

"Shut up, Morton."

"I'm out." Doc flings in his cards. "Come on, man. You did kick ass. Nothing to be shy about. He's just telling it like it is."

Pinky looks at Simmons, studies him for a second. "Your two and two more." Into the pot go four more dollars. He looks at Doc. "Enough. It doesn't matter now." Turns to me, but his eyes go to Simmons, "Four to you."

Four to me. With only Jacks? Two raisers? Shit, no! "I'm out." Flip my cards into the pot.

"Yes, it does." Davis presses Pinky.

Simmons covers his cards with his hand, taps them with his index finger.

"It always matters when you blow away gooks."

Doc stares at Davis and Pinky.

Simmons looks at Pinky, stops tapping his cards, peels up a corner of each card, takes a peek at them, makes sure he has what he thinks he has. Or feigns insecurity.

Pinky scowls at Davis. "No, it doesn't." Back to Simmons, "Shit or get off the pot."

"I'll shit, funny guy. Call. How many?"

"Two."

"Two for the pigeon." He flings two cards to Pinky after he discards two.

Pigeon, my ass. He's got three of something.

Doc to Davis, "Change the subject."

"Dealer takes two." Simmons slides two cards, one at a time off the deck, sets them down next to his cards on the table, plunks the deck onto the pot.

"How long you been in country?"

Doc and Davis are in their own little game. I'm in both.

"Eight months. Why?" Davis looks imposed upon.

"Seen any action?" Doc presses the issue.

Simmons picks up his hand, pulls out two cards, flings them to the discarded deck of cards.

"I've splattered my share of gooks. Got a nice collection of ears."

"I see." Doc's eyes flare up. His look burns a hole through Davis. He shows great restraint. Pinky shakes his head, keeps his eyes on his cards.

Simmons picks up his two draw cards, one at time, very carefully, puts them with the three remaining cards in his hand. Shuffles them, top card to the bottom, nonstop. "Well, Mr. Openers?"

Pinky raises his eyes over his cards to Simmons. "Check."

Still shuffling his cards, Simmons smiles at Pinky. Takes a peek at his cards, puts them on the table, face down. He digs through his money, finds a five, flings it into the pot. "Five."

"How were the women doing back in the World when you left?" *Way to go, Doc. We all like to talk about women.*

"They were as sweet as…."

"Your five and five more."

Now it is a balls-out game. Doc, Davis, and I turn our attention to the duel between Simmons and Pinky.

All eyes on Simmons. He does not look so confident now. Shakes his head. He believes Pinky got him. I know he does.

"Fold." He slams his cards into the pot.

"Openers." Pinky turns over a pair of Kings, buries the other three cards into the discards at the center of the table.

"Have the third one?" It kills Simmons, not knowing.

"You should have ponied up the five if you really wanted to know."

Knowing Pinky, I know he had it.

"Your deal, Doc."

Pinky rakes in his winnings. Doc gathers up the cards, straightens and shuffles them.

"I met this one gal about a month before I shipped out. The E-Club, Pendleton."

Davis is back talking about women back in the World. Good.

Doc continues shuffling. "Ante up."

We throw in our dollars.

Davis continues. "She was drinking a rum and coke. They all seem to like rum and coke. Why do they like rum and coke?"

He leans in to the center of the table, expecting an answer. No one does. He leans back in his chair. "A little on the plump side. A nice, soft ride."

"Are you going to wear the spots off those cards or deal?" Simmons is impatient.

"Maybe." Doc pays more attention to Davis' chatter than to his shuffling.

"Not a knockout, but good looking. Dark hair, chocolate eyes."

"Interesting. Doesn't sound too bad."

"She wasn't. Get this. She drove a '57 Ford two door station wagon. I never saw one before. Practical car. If you know what I mean."

Smiles of understanding.

Yeah. I know. I got one, too. Love it.

Doc stops shuffling.

"Got her number? Maybe I can hook up with her when I get stateside."

"I don't know, Doc. She's married and her old man's over here somewhere. She doesn't know when he'll come home. Might be risky. I lucked out and got out of Dodge before he got back."

"I'll take my chances."

"Diane. Don't remember her last name."

Doc deals the cards.

"From San Diego." Davis looks at his cards. "Not me."

Pinky puts his cards face down on the table, crosses his arms. "Me, either."

Shit cards. "By me."

"Don't look at me. Pass." Simmons turns to Doc.

"Boy, can I fucking deal or what?" Doc slams his cards onto the deck.

We toss our cards toward Davis. He gathers them up and puts them with the deck.

It's his deal.

"That Diane was a lot of fun. She might be in a world of shit if her hubby finds out about her entertaining the troops." He shuffles the cards.

"Olsen. That's her name. Diane Olsen."

Olsen? That's Diane's maiden name!

"Shut the fuck up and deal the goddam motherfucking cards!"

R & R

Notice

TO THE COMM bunker after evening chow. Start my radio watch an hour early.
Give Lucero an extra hour off. He has time to get some of the evening chow
before it gets cold. It won't be C-rats or whatever else he can scrounge up.

Enjoyment of the quiet, calm, well protected comm bunker is what I need.
Read. Maybe write some letters home. No word from Diane. Write her. For
sure.

A look at the ambush schedule shows Papa One out at 1945, Papa Two at
2200, Papa Three and Papa Six 0100.

That's it. I'll be in the rack by the time Three and Six go out in search of the
bad guys. *Good hunting, guys. Safe hunting.*

"Tiger Papa net. Tiger Papa net. Tiger Papa. Sit rep. Over."

"Papa One, good here. Out."

"Papa Two, all secure. Out."

"Papa Three, same-same. Out."

"Papa Six, ditto. Out."

"Tiger Papa. Roger. Thanks, guys. Papa out."

Lean back in the lawn chair, gaze at the map of the DMZ. The safe, quiet
of the bunker envelops me. My thoughts go to home.

"Morton."

Instantly, I am back to this shit hole.

I look up. It's Pinky.

"You're married, right?"

"Yeah."

"Got an R & R to Hawaii available if you're interested."

"Fuck yeah, I'm interested."

"You can leave as soon as you're ready. Do you want to draw any of your pay?"

"All of it."

Call Diane. No. Airline reservations. Then call her. Bitchin. See Diane. Have some sex, a lot of sex, surf, eat, drink and be merry, more fun in the sack, and surf some more. Later, Nam.

On the MARS horn. Make the reservations. Call Diane.

"Hi, Diane. It's me."

"Oh. Hi."

"How're you doing?"

"Fine. You? All healed up?"

"Yeah. Listen. I don't have much time for this call."

"Yeah?" *Where is she? Sounds distant.*

"I got R & R to Hawaii. You get to join me. You fly out the 21st. I'll meet you at the airport there."

"Great." *That's it for enthusiasm?*

My heel bounces up and down. "I thought you'd like that, Hawaii. Be excited."

"Yes. Hawaii. I am excited." *Jeez. Don't be like that. Karen wouldn't be.*

"Don't you want to see me?" *Karen would. Stop it, Tom!*

"Sure."

"Something wrong?" I drum my fingers on the table.

"Nope."

Sounds like there is. "Ok." *What next?* "See you in Hawaii."

"Yeah, fine."

What? "Love you, babe." Shake my head. *Do I, really?*

"Yeah. Me, too." *Do you? Doesn't sound like it.* "Bye."

"Good-bye."

Hang up.

I sigh. Big.

What the hell was that all about? She seemed far away. Distant. Indifferent. Cold really. Unemotional. Odd. Not much to say. Our first anniversary and I get that shit? She doesn't get it. Maybe she is getting it. There. Maybe Davis did know her.

Fuck it. Just wait and see.

Deep breath.

At least, it's a sure piece of ass.

No Letter

P-HQ Cam Lo

8 Feb 68

Dear Val,

I thought I'd better write you to let you know that I am fine and that there won't be any letter. You probably already know I'm at Cam Lo District Headquarters now, and that I was here the 2nd Feb. when all those NVA tried to overrun us. Well, all the guys from P-5 were pulled back to P- HQ. and were here during the attack. The letter that was written was lost or burned in the attack. Also some of the guys that signed are not with us anymore, if you know what I mean. A few of the others were wounded real bad and were sent home or to Cam Ranh Bay. You can tell the girls what I just told you or you don't have to if you don't want. But do tell them that everyone really enjoyed and appreciated them. They all wanted to be sure that their thanks was conveyed to you girls. Here's a couple guys are still around:

> *Cpl. William LeFevre*
> *same address*
> *CAC P-2*
> *Cpl. GJ Callahan*
> *P-6*

These are some snipers that were there:

> *HQ. CO. 3rd Marines 3rd MarDiv*
> *Sniper Platoon*
> *L/Cpl. JJ Johnson*
> *Pfc. Puckett*
> *Pfc. Thatcher*

L/Cpl. Blevins

Pfc. Lopez

I'm sure some of these guys will appreciate a line. Tell them I'm sorry there's no letter. But, I felt it should have been a unit thing, but the unit is no longer a unit. I lost some good friends, Val, people I'll always remember. One was Doc Young, our Corpsman. He was one of the most liked and admired men of our unit. We just got the word yesterday that he died in the morning from his wounds. He's been put up for the Silver Star for his performance during the attack.

I've got R&R to Hawaii for 20th of February. Diane's supposed to come out to meet me. I leave here on the 17th and dig this—they're supposed to attack this place again sometime between now and February 17th! Boy!

Talking about old friends, I haven't gotten Barbara's letter yet. I got a letter from Tom Van Wagner day before yesterday. I also have gotten letters from Dave Pollard and Bobby. Tom told me Gordy went into the Air Force and Debbie got married! Ha! Ha!

Guess who I bumped in to over here. Jack Bivens! Remember him from Helix? He's with the company that's here to reinforce this compound. He joined in July '67 and he's a Pfc. He's been in Nam for about two months. He's a machine gunner. Congrats for graduating. What are you going to do now?

Also—happy belated birthday—sorry I missed it, but I think you understand the circumstances.

Mom has some of the details about the attack. Like I told her, I can give you guys the whole story when I get back. Save all the articles you come across about the attack on Cam Lo 2 Feb.

There's a guy, Larry Eades, that is writing you. He goes home late this month. He'll try to call you. If he does and he's in town, how about having him over for dinner? Well, Val, I'll close for now. Write when you can. Be good.

Love,

Tommy

Cam Lo to Hawaii

PINKY MAKES ALL the arrangements. Our 3/4 ton PC transports me to Dong Ha. I hop a C-123 flight to Danang. It is nice to fly out of Dong Ha not under fire like when I arrived last October.

Excitement builds when we land. Check-in, find the barracks. Unpack. Get my service khakis cleaned and pressed. Mount my ribbons over the left breast pocket. Hang it up in my locker, next to my rack.

One day to kill in Danang before heading to Hawaii. I spend it in the E-Club, drink ice cold beer in relative safety, enjoy the hell out of myself with others on their way to R & R. Get ready for R & R. With Diane. In Hawaii.

Still the sounds of war, though distant, remind me of what I escape. Temporarily.

Hawaii. The beer's colder, tastes better, I'm sure. Screwdrivers? Yeah. Screwdrivers, too. Quiet, no war sounds, no war. Rum and cokes for Diane. Paradise and Diane. Diane. She sounded different, distant. Why? Anything to do with Davis? Not so sure about her anymore. Should trust her. I don't know. And what about me?

Chug another swig of beer. Pound down more drinks. Laugh more. Get wasted. Enjoy it, no matter what.

Give her the benefit of the doubt.

0600

Wiped out, with a pounding head and blurry eyes, I do the three Ss. A peek in the mirror tells me my eyes are so bloodshot, if I scratch them, I will bleed to death. After putting on my uniform, I check myself out in a mirror. *Spiffy.* Better than my jungles, flak jacket, and steel pot. Not needed where I'm going.

The thought of breakfast gags me. I pack up my gear. Weave my way to the waiting area in the terminal. I catch a few ZZZs before they call for boarding. Ascending the portable stairs is more difficult than it should be.

Doesn't matter. Hawaii and Diane will make it all better. I hope.

Plop my ass down in the first available seat. Look around the cabin, see we all appear to be in the same shape. *Too much to drink last night? Yup.*

The stewardesses are stunning. They look sharper in their uniforms than we do in ours.

Nice breasts. Tight butts. And, all are round eyes. Pretty faces. They look younger than we do. Just how old do you have to be to be a stewardess?

The plane gets airborne. We clap.

FUCK OFF, VIET NAM!

Arrival

OUR UNITED FLIGHT lands in Hawaii.

0900

Fort DeRussy for processing. None of us wastes any time beating feet into Honolulu after the REMFs dot the Is and cross the Ts, and unleash us.

Rain pelts me as I stride toward town. Doesn't bother me. The rain is the same temperature as the air. Funny thing about this rain. It doesn't block out the sunshine. It doesn't get darker. It is still bright out. Besides, I am away from Nam and in Hawaii. I will spend five days with Diane. *Cool.*

Up ahead I see painted on the side of the building, THE ROMANY CLUB. First stop, the Romany Club. It may be only 1100, but I still want a drink. A real drink. An American drink. A screwdriver, tall.

I step into the club. Before my eyes adjust to the darkness, I find a table, sit down, and place my duffle bag down at my feet.

Before I know it, a soft, feminine voice breathes into my ear, "What would you like?" Her accent huskies up her voice. *Australian?*

I turn to the voice and come face-to-face with swaying twin oval, khaki tan objects, each tipped with a darker shade of brown.

Wow! Boobs! Nice boobs!

The temptation to cup them in my hands is immediate. My decision not to is almost as immediate.

I tilt my head back and see the smiling face of a topless cocktail waitress. The only things she wears above her waist are two dangling gold hoop earrings. Her hair, a soothing blonde shade, hangs just below her ears, golden brown eyes that twinkle, slim pink lips, and a thin nose adorn her slender face. Her smile shines bright white with almost straight teeth. One more glance at her boobs, then back to her eyes.

"What I want, I can"t have, so I'll settle for a screwdriver, tall."

A smile, a wink, "I'll be right back."

She turns and scurries away. Her cute, taunt, little butt follows. Goes nicely with her boobs. *Choice package.*

She places my drink on the table. Admiring her breasts, I slide a twenty to her.

"Keep 'em coming. When this runs out, let me know. Save some for yourself."

A pause, "Thank you. I'm Noelle." *A Christmas package I want under my tree.*

"Corporal...." *not here,* "Tom."

"Glad to meet you. Tom."

"The pleasure is all mine."

Exchange grins. She leaves to attend to the few customers in the place.

A big swallow of my screwdriver.

Get an apartment. Pick up Diane at the airport at four. Get some civvies? Wait for Diane first? I got time. For many screwdrivers. Much okane.

Two drinks later, "Any places you can recommend to stay for five days?"

Noelle sets down my fourth drink. Then, juts her hip out and holds her tray on it. Her boobs sit there begging for attention. *I'm willing. Be good.*

"We have a list by the door. I'll get you one."

She returns with it. Then off she goes. Again.

I scan the list. The dimness keeps me from reading it. I down my last, for now, screwdriver. When I get up, Noelle appears.

"Don't just leave yet. You have change coming."

"Keep it on a tab. I'll be back after I find a place. That change won't last long. I'll make another deposit on it."

"Okay, then."

I amble out.

A place four blocks from the Romany meets my needs. Fifth floor, studio, shower, small kitchen, a window with a view of nothing but surrounding buildings. *Not going to look out the window much.*

To make sure Diane is on her way, I call her mother. After pleasantries, before I ask, she puts Diane on the phone.

"What are you doing there? Why aren't you on the plane? I'm waiting for you."

"I can't make it."

"What do you mean you can't make it?"

"I got a job at Longs. I'm working tonight."

"The hell you are. You call them and tell them you quit. Pack. I'll call back and tell you what time the next plane leaves." I'm pissed off.

"But...."

"No fucking buts. Get to it."

"Okay. Okay."

We hang up, without pleasantries. *What a fucking pisser.*

Arrangements and phone call completed, back to the Romany Club and Noelle. No need for my eyes to adjust. I know what to expect. No surprises. Only Noelle. All of her.

She sees me. Waves. *I'm in love.*

Return her wave, sit down at my table. Wait for my drink and Noelle.

"We have a Belly Dancer show in the back room. Nine o'clock and again at eleven. I think you'd enjoy it."

"I'll check it out."

Blitzed, I stagger out of the Club. Find my condo. Crash.

9:00 Show

I SHOW UP early enough to get a front row seat, next to the stage. The show is free, except for the two drink minimum. Order my usual. Screwdriver, tall.

One sip slides down just before the music starts. The introduction made, out she comes, Fatima, or whatever her name is. She is beautiful, exotic. Her colorful costume dark and bright, red, yellow, black, green and orange. The colors complement her light olive complexion, green eyes, jet black hair and full red lips that beckon from behind a veil. Kissing them preys on my mind. Though covered head to toe, I see she has a body that won't quit.

She starts swinging around the stage, her body moves with the music, wafting her silky scarf outfit around her. I hear bells, but not bells. Tiny cymbals adorn her fingers. They make the bell sounds. The moving picture painted on the stage mesmerizes me. I cannot look away. I am unable to take a hit off my screwdriver. I may not make the two drink minimum at this rate.

How does she move like that, flowing so fluidly?

Sensuality shines through every move, every sway, every bump, each undulation.

I need a sip of my drink. Instead of a sip, I gulp it down, leave only ice in the glass.

My attention goes back on her. I barely notice another drink set down in front of me. Ogling her entrancing performance takes precedence over any drink.

Lots of hoots, hollers, claps from the audience. I am powerless to hoot, holler, or clap. I can't even blink.

Where has she been all my life? Nowhere near you, stupid.

She moves up close to the edge of the stage. Closer to us front-row-seat-holders.

Rippling around the horseshoe-shaped stage, she looks down at each guy. When she gets to me, I gasp for air, take a deep breath, take a big hit off my drink. Her glistening emerald-green eyes draw mine into hers. She spins around, turns her back to me. I am grateful for the break of our eye contact. I gulp down the rest of my drink. She turns around. Her lips flash a tiny smile through her veil. They are parted as if she just blew me a kiss. She moves on around the stage.

The place goes crazy as she strips off her scarves, veil, all the way down to her skimpy belly dancer outfit. I am frozen. She is more beautiful and sexy than I imagine. Her high cheekbones, once hidden behind the veil, underscore her eyes. They sit above fiery red lips, perfectly. Her figure is full. A woman's figure, full-not-fat. All the curves in all the right places. Not hidden. Displayed in perfect proportions. Her neck slopes down to her shoulders in sleek lines. Her breasts, as big and round as overgrown casaba melons, put a strain on her armor-look bra. They sit solidly above a not-too-thin waist line. A green jewel, planted in her bellybutton, accents her continuously pulsating midsection. The waistband of her pantaloons sits well below the jewel and her hip bones. Only skin as smooth-as-a-virgin's-thigh spans the area between her bra and waistband. She turns around revealing pronounced twin dimples in the small of her back, just above the waistband. Her butt coordinates with all her movements. It doesn't so much shake as it quivers. It complements her figure and breasts in size, firmness, proportion.

All her features dance to the beat of the music. I feel as if my eyes are about to bounce out of their sockets and bleed.

She dances a long time that goes by in a flash. The music stops. So does she. The roar of the audience reaches a head numbing crescendo. I imagine not a single heart in this room beats. Mine stands still. Suck in a sharp breath. Heart restarts, not beat. Pounds. I blink. I grin.

That was bitchin.

She glides around the stage, graciously accepting our accolades.

"I need a volunteer for my favorite part of the show." She moves in my direction. She stops in front of me. I can barely see her face above her breasts.

"How about you?"

I can't react, rigor mortis sets in.

She bends down. Presses her face against mine and whispers, "I promise I won't disrespect the uniform."

Her words barely register. I enjoy the view of her cavernous cleavage. So close, I can feel my breath bounce back at me.

She takes my hand and leads me onto the stage. We walk across the stage. She presses up against me.

"Don't worry. Everything will be okay." Her voice is husky, mysterious.

Oh, I hope so.

We get to a platform in the middle of the stage. It is just big enough for one person to sit.

She pats it. "Have a seat. Legs straight out."

Easy enough.

I have a seat, as instructed.

She pulsates around me a couple times. Stops in front of me. Out comes a kazoo. From I don't know where. *Oh-oh.*

She hands it to me. "All you have to do is play this."

"Okay."

"Nonstop for a few minutes."

Snickers from the crowd ooze into my ears.

"Okay."

"No matter what happens, keep playing, with both hands on it at all times."

Chuckles replace the snickers.

I swallow hard.

Music starts. She dances. I play the kazoo. She twirls around me. Eyes on her, both hands on the kazoo, I play.

I lose sight of her as she moves behind me. Something soft and pillowy brushes against my back, circles round and round, up and down, over my back, to my neck, comes to rest atop my head, shakes back and forth a few times, then is gone.

Oh shit! Her tits. They feel terrific. Must be cloud nine.

She comes into view once again, at my side. Dances. Still, I play the kazoo. Her back is to me. Pressed against my arm, she shimmies and shakes, moves up and down my arm like a bear scratching its back on a sturdy tree.

She wiggles her ass against me. Turns around, shakes her tits near my head. I keep playing. Leaning forward over my lap, those tantalizing tits nearly knock the kazoo out of my mouth, through my hands. *Keep playing, keep hands here, away from her, play, play, play!*

She straddles me. My kazoo playing continues. She leans back. She pulsates. Her tits quiver. I play. Her sultry eyes sear a hungry look at me. Penetrates right into my inner core.

Harder, Tom. Play harder!

No matter where my eyes land on her, I can't stop fantasizing about the lovely lady in front of me. She dances. She throbs. She quivers. She shakes and shimmies. All parts move. She drives me crazy.

All I can do is continue playing the damn kazoo.

In continuous motion, she glides her way around me, twists and twirls, bumps and jiggles, makes my eyes open wider and wider. She stops at my feet.

I play my little about-to-burst heart out.

The music fades out. She grinds to a halt. I keep playing. To be safe.

The crowd, once again, makes the room shake with applause, hoots and hollers, and whistles.

"Very good. You can stop now." She whispers in my ear. Her moist, hot breath raises goosebumps. She moves away, flashes a smile. I smile back, sheepishly.

She helps me off the platform. Takes my hand, leads me off the stage. Before she lets go, she turns to me, pulls me close. Her eyes reflect a mischievous look.

"My last show is at eleven. Why don't you come back for the show? Afterwards, we can…." she grins, "….get a drink."

I can barely hear her over the noise. *Damn.*

"I'd love to, but I'm picking up my wife at the airport at eleven."

With a sad, innocent look, "Too bad." She kisses me on the cheek, turns, and exits through the back curtain. What remains of her costume trails her, wafts through the air.

I turn to the still wild and loud crowd. My arms go up in triumph. Thunderous approval rocks the room.

As I exit, they pat me on the back.

"Way to go, man."

"Wow."

Some shake my hand.

"How'd you do it?"

"What was it like?"

"No way I could do that."

All smiles, wide-eyed with envy. I grin. And keep walking.

A drink. I need a drink.

At the bar, "Screwdriver, tall."

The bartender, another topless honey, produces it, sets it down on a cocktail napkin in front of me, takes my money.

"Keep the change."

Cocks her head, smiles, then she's gone. Way too fast. I enjoy the full view that is her and her endowments.

All too soon, and three screwdrivers later. *Fuck. Time to get moving. Gotta pick her up. She better be there. Or what, fool?*

Outside, taxis line up to take us, the booze laden patrons of the Romany Club Belly Dance Show, to wherever.

"Airport." I slide into the taxi.

"Yes, Sir!"

We're off.

"Picking someone up?"

"Yeah." *Dammit.*

"You stationed here?"

"No. R and R."

"I see."

The rest of the way is quiet. Neither of us says another word. I am alone, in the quiet, with my thoughts.

What if she's not on the plane? Will I have time to get back to the Romany Club? To my belly dancer? Can we still get that drink? Will she want to? What to do if Diane is not on the plane? Figure something out. After many 'drivers? I like this place. Hate to go back. The Nam. Fuck! Stay here. Enjoy now. Wait and see, Morton. Maybe she'll be on the plane and we'll have a good time. Give her the benefit of the doubt.

She Arrives

DIANE APPROACHES THROUGH the gate. I hurry toward her. Her pace is slow, does not change. Mine quickens. She wears a loose-fitting muumuu. Unrevealing. That's okay. I know what's under there.

Her raven hair is shorter than I remember. Her brown eyes look tired. Her face bears a wan smile.

We share a little kiss.

"Hi, honey."

"Hi," she mumbles.

No running into each other's arms? No passionate kiss? This is not a 1940's romance movie, numbskull. It was a long flight. She's tired. Not as tired as she's going to be.

We pick up her luggage, one small suitcase. Climb into a taxi. Start for the condo.

"How was your flight?"

"Long." *No shit, Sherlock.*

"Did you get any rest or sleep?"

"No. Too much on my mind."

"Like?"

"Having to quit my job to come here. Finding another job when I get home."

"Sorry about that. I just thought we should be together for our first anniversary."

"Oh, yeah."

All the while she looks out the window, not at me.

Neither one of us says anything more.

Hot fucking diggity. Another cab ride in silence. Well, at least I'll have a good time at the condo. A good fuck, anyway. If she puts her heart into it.

She opens her suitcase, pulls out some things, rushes into the bathroom, and closes the door behind her. She showers. Alone.

I wait on the bed. She comes out of the bathroom wearing her favorite sleepwear. Baby dolls.

You won't be wearing them long.

"Want a drink?"

"No. I'm really tired. I just want to go to sleep." She flops onto the bed.

She turns to me as I snuggle up to her. I kiss her. She kisses me back. Sort of. Removing her baby dolls is like being in the backseat of a car, trying to get the clothes off a reluctant date.

Finally, we have sex. No. We fuck. I fuck. I don't know what she does. Mostly nothing. Not like before. And I am not sure I really care. I'm as satisfied as I can be under the circumstances.

Fuck her.

I roll off her. She turns away. Falls asleep. On my back, I stare up through the ceiling, through the floors above me, through the roof, to the sky. Unfocused.

Guess that's what sex with a cadaver is like. Only, she's warm to the touch. To hell with her. I got mine. Maybe she's just tired? That's not it. Whatever. I'm going to have a good time here. Could've been with Fatima? Maybe. Now, I'm stuck with Diane. Ahh, she's just tired.

She perks up in the morning. We have a reasonably good time. At least, I do. She seems to enjoy herself. I don't know what to think.

We shop the International Marketplace. I get swim trunks, civvies, and touristy stuff. And a camera. Lots of pictures to take. She is not keen on having her picture taken.

We rent a motorcycle, go up to Diamondhead.

I surf.

She sunbathes.

For our anniversary, we go to a luau. Show great. Food good. Company so-so.

I surf some more.

She swims.

The Don Ho Show exudes warmth. Tiny bubbles fun. She laughs and smiles. Not at me. I have a good time anyway.

Surfing is my main activity.

She shops. With my money.

We eat a lot. Drink a lot. I drink the most. Make love not at all. Have sex a lot. Actually, we fuck a lot.

In the cab on the way to the airport, "Have a good time?"

"I guess so."

My jaw tightens. "See you in a few months." *Maybe?* I look out the window.

"Okay." *That's it? Just okay?*

"Fine." I just want to smack her one.

The rest of the way is another silent taxi ride.

I check in her suitcase. We walk out to the boarding area. I try to kiss her. She turns her cheek to me.

"What the fuck? You pissed about something? What's with you?"

"Nothing. Really. I'm sorry. I'll see you when you get back."

Back? Not home? Shit. That's right. You will see me when I get back. We'll see what happens. It don't look good.

We turn and walk away from each other.

She di hoa ky.

I di fucking Viet Nam.

Pinky asks if I would like to go on R & R to Australia. I would have to leave in five days.

Shit. I'm tapped out. "Can't. Got no money."

"Too bad. I hear they love Americans there." Walks away.

Was it worth it? Going to Hawaii? Don't think so.

Australia would have been better.

Back in the Nam

The Skipper

MY CO, LIEUTENANT Bushrod, differs from others I serve under. They are not all alike. Some are cut out to lead, some are not. Some learn to lead. Lieutenant Bushrod is not cut out and does not learn to lead. We tolerate him, dub him Aiming Stake. He doesn't know. Goofy and immature, his decision making skills leave a lot to be desired.

One of our units gets into a firefight. They direct mortar fire via the radio. From our Command Center at HQ, the Lieutenant tries to cut in. He wants a report. I grab the handset from him, "They're in the shit and you're fucking them over, cutting in. They need a clear channel to direct the mortars. They'll report when it's over."

He stares at me like a precocious child that's just been told No.

After the firefight, they mop up, then give him a full report.

A month later, he accompanies that same unit on a night ambush. A firefight erupts. The squad leader requests mortar fire. He barely finishes, when Aiming Stake comes on the radio, voice three octaves higher, repeats the request. When the firefight is over, I key the handset and say, "See how it works now?"

The next morning, when he returns to HQ, he looks at me and grimaces.

We get word about a missing trailer. A villager turned it upside down to use as a roof for his bunker. The Lieutenant has me run security for him to pick it up. Pinky drives the PC. With the canvas top down, the cab is open air. We retrieve the trailer bed and put it in the bed of the PC. I ride on top. Lieutenant Bushrod stands up in the cab holding onto the frame of the windshield. As we drive through the village, on our way back to HQ, we pass a couple guys from our unit walking in the opposite direction. As we pass them, they turn and look at me. I mouth, "Watch this."

In my finest military voice, "PASSS IN REVUUUUE!"

The Lieutenant springs to attention, holds onto the frame with his left hand, salutes with his right hand, turns his head from side to side. The guys bend over in laughter.

Time nears for him to rotate back to the World. He sits on his rack at night, stares at a brochure for a Jaguar XKE, goes through the gears. He pantomimes the action, hand motions and the clutch-gas pedal foot movements.

"Rooooom, varooooom, vrooooom, rooooooommmmm!"

Way to go, Stake. 0 to 60 in 8 seconds flat.

His orders arrive, identify his next duty station as Iceland. We fill his head with visions of continuous snow and blizzards with snowdrifts of ten feet, nothing but ice.

"That's why it's called Iceland, Lieutenant."

He believes us so much he writes his daddy for information. Travel brochures arrive ten days later. Relief replaces the alarm that shows on his face. He can still buy his XKE.

He celebrates his twenty-fifth birthday with us. Several birthday cards adorn shelves next to his rack. When he isn't around, we peak inside the cards. One has a written note, in a feminine hand, that reads, "Happy 25th birthday, Mason! I'll bet you still don't look a day over 18! Love, Rebecca."

That sums him up.

Hitching a Ride

THE TANK RUMBLES to a halt. Ledford and I hop down. Start out for the LZ.

"I don't want ever to do that again."

"They say they need us because we worked the area and know the people. What a crock of crap. They didn't need us or use us for anything on their stupid little sweep. Nothing."

Ledford looks disgruntled.

"The only thing that was good about the sweep was seeing that kid again."

"No shit. Doc did a good job."

"If I didn't know where that cut was, I wouldn't have been able to see the scar."

"I hated to tell her parents about Doc. Broke them up pretty bad."

"Them crying is what I hated."

"I wish they hadn't asked about him."

"Too bad Doc didn't get to see the results of his handiwork."

"Roger that," a quick look at him. "You look awful."

"So do you, Kemosabe."

We stop. Look at each other. Sweat and caked brown-gray dirt masks his face. Shredded uniform hangs from his thin frame. Scratches with dried blood on bare skin.

His look tells me I must look like he does. Chuckles. Continue our trek to the LZ.

Choppers, rotors twirling, line a grassy area near the perimeter of Camp Carroll. Marines stand around, wait for flights to wherever. Chaos.

The Wop—Wop—Wop of the choppers muffles all other sounds.

Ledford nudges me. Thumbs in the direction of the choppers. I look. Give him a shrug.

He points. A closer look reveals a radioman sits on a lawn chair, handset to his ear.

Must be the controller running this mess.

Ledford acknowledges my look to him.

Need to hitch a ride to Cam Lo District HQ.

I stroll over to the radioman. Tap him on the shoulder. "You assigning flights?"

He looks up at me. Lowers the handset. "Yeah. Wait one." He looks down to his clipboard. Handset to ear. "Beetle 6. You're clear. Go."

Whine of engine revving. Beat of rotor blades swooshing through the air speeds up.

A chopper lifts off, banks to the south.

Controller looks up from his clipboard. Stays seated. "How many to where?"

"Two. Cam Lo District Headquarters."

"Okay. Be a while."

"Fine."

Ledford joins me.

A couple minutes pass.

"This is taking way too long," Ledford mutters in my ear.

I steal up close to the controller, look over his shoulder, focus on the frequency dial.

Gotcha.

Return to Ledford. He looks puzzled.

Pick up my radio, one strap over my shoulder. Switch on radio. Dial in the frequency I just acquired. Wink at Ledford.

"Good idea, Mort."

Handset to my ear. Wait for the network to clear. "Any chopper. Any chopper. This is Tiger Papa. This is Tiger Papa. Over."

The controller's head pops up. Handset to ear. Looks around.

Ledford steps between him and me. Turns to me, does a Groucho eyebrow lift. Smiles.

I wink back.

"Any chopper, this is Tiger Papa. Over."

"Tiger Papa. Chaucer One. Over." *Please be a pilot.*

Controller stands up. Scans the LZ. Handset remains at ear.

I turn my back to him.

"Chaucer One, Tiger Papa. Need a lift for two to Cam Lo District Headquarters. Over."

"That controller guy is going nuts," Ledford snickers in my ear.

"Where's that? Over." *Sounds like a pilot.*

"Between here and Dong Ha on Route 9. Over."

"Can you spot it from the air? Over."

"Affirmative. Over."

"Roger. Where are you? Over."

"Behind the controller, hand up. Over."

"Gotcha. See me? Over." A stretched out arm waves back and forth.

"Affirm. Tiger Papa out."

"Chaucer One, Out."

I tap Ledford's shoulder, point to chopper.

We double-time to it.

"Hey!" The controller bellows at us.

Our response as we hop aboard is a smart-ass wave and smile.

The chopper lifts off.

"Point it out." The crew chief yells into my ear.

I nod. Lean out of hatch. Hold on to bulkhead. *Do not let go. Not a good way to buy it.*

We cruise east over Route 9.

"What's their freq?"

I tell him. He nods. Speaks into his headset.

Resume looking down the road. Wind screeches through my ears. Jostles my hair.

So, this is what a fighter pilot sees.

Group of buildings appears in the distance. Juts out from the barren ground, on both sides of Route 9.

Get crew chief's attention, jab my index finger in the air toward the compound.

Thumb up, he speaks into headset. Motions us to come close.

"We're not setting down."

Ledford and I dart looks at each other.

"Compound under rocket attack. When I tell you, jump."

"From how high?"

"It'll be okay." His smile peers out from behind the microphone of his headset.

Is everything funny to you airedales?

The chopper circles then dives in a tight spiral to the south side of the compound. The deck races up to greet us. Chopper comes to a halt, hovers.

"Go! Go! Go!"

Glance down.

What the fuck? Too far down! Aw, fuck it.

Side by side, Ledford and I leap. As we slam to the deck, dirt kicks up when the chopper zooms off.

Rocket explosions drown out the roar of the fleeing chopper.

Crouched, we scramble north, across Route 9.

A rocket scores a hit on the RC292 I erected the day before we left on the sweep.

Ledford vanishes down the stairs into the bunker.

I watch my RC292 disintegrate.

Shake my fist in the air.

"You sons of bitches."

"Get down here, Morton."

Dammit.

Dive into the bunker. Skid to a stop at Ledford's feet.

"Ah. Poor Morty." He smiles down at me. "Got your pretty new antenna, did they?"

Extends hand. I grab it. He pulls me up.

"Yeah. The assholes."

We burst out laughing.

Close Call

"I'M GOING INTO the ville for a Coke. Anyone want to go?"

No one answers.

Good. I'll be alone with her.

She opens her house to us as a Coca-Cola bar. The Cokes are not cold, just cool. With her broken English and my fractured Vietnamese, we will talk about nothing.

Every time I have been there with the guys, she gives me more attention than she does the others. She stands barely five feet tall. Her smile radiates from her round-trying-to-be-oval face. Other features include creamy tan skin, dark lips longing to kiss and be kissed, a cute Gidget nose, and, if not deep, dark brown, then midnight black eyes. Her hair hangs down past her shoulders and smells different. Not bad, just different. Pleasant. Sexy.

Hewn from her peasant family's rice paddies, she ripened into a classic French-Vietnamese beauty.

Her eyes dance when she looks at me. She is not flirting. Or is she? Rumor has it she is married to an ARVN Lieutenant. Each time I leave, she touches my arm and says, "You come back."

I do, but never alone. Always with others.

This time, only me.

She lets me in then drifts across the room to the far wall. One look at each other, we both know what we want. We know what is going to happen. I slide the door shut, latch it, go to her.

As we kiss, she clutches my wrist, guides my hand into her pants, under her panties, and on down. There is no doubt what she feels and wants. We move to the bed. As we lower ourselves onto it, she whispers, "No."

"Tai sao?"

"Dong Bau see."

"Bunker?"

She nods, then kisses me.

We move to the bunker. She gets on all fours and starts to crawl in. I follow close behind. Toss my M16 up against one wall. I strip her pants and panties off her. She rolls over onto her back, offers herself up to me, one foot up on the wall beside her. As I go to her, she lifts her tunic over her tits. They are creamy brown with dark, erect nipples. Her body is firm, taut, skin soft, smooth. Her hands are gentle. Her touch, tender.

We fuck, have sex, make love. I don't know what to call it. She's wonderful, hot, exciting, sensual, sensational, active, flexible, enthusiastic.

Wow!

Then, it is over.

I roll off her onto my back, onto my M16. She turns to face me, my arm slides around her. We lay there a few minutes. Her, me, and my M16.

"We go now."

She starts to get dressed. Before she puts on her panties, I take them from her, "You souvenir me?"

She smiles. I put them into a pocket of my trousers.

We crawl from the bunker into the house. She pulls on her pants. I adjust my jungles. Then, sit in one of the chairs in the main room. She brings me a Coke. She smiles a soft smile. I feel as if I grin. A sip of Coke removes the grin. I smile back at her.

I'm in love. Stop it, you idiot. It's only a fabulous fuck, a nice piece of ass.

I down my Coke. *Get out of here, Tom.*

She grabs my arm. I turn to her. She kisses me.

It's not me she wants. Di Hao Ky. That's what she wants. Should I? Maybe? Nope. Can't do it. Won't do it. It was good. That's all. Besides what do I do with Diane?

Get the hell out of here. NOW. And don't come back.

Di di mau back to the compound.

Into my hooch, my haven. Akins lounges on his cot, reads.

"Hey, Akins. Here." I toss the panties to him. He catches them.

"Your girlfriend souvenir me after our romp in her bunker. Man, she's something else, isn't she?" I laugh. But I know it is not all that funny to Akins. "Still want to marry her? Take her home to the World?"

He bolts off his cot toward me. James grabs him. "Don't. It's not worth it. The gook bitch ain't worth it."

Akins glares at me, "I guess not."

He goes back to his cot and tosses the panties back to me. He lays down, hands behind his head.

I shit-can the panties.

I helped Akins dodge a bullet.

I may have dodged one myself

Romeo Foxtrot November

THE LIEUTENANT OF the platoon assigned to Cam Lo District Headquarters looks upset.

"Raise Papa 1."

"Yes, Sir."

"I want to talk to my squad leader."

"Yes, Sir." Pick up the handset, "Tiger Papa One, Tiger Papa, over."

"One, go."

"Kilo 6 Actual wants to talk to Kilo 6 Alpha, over."

"Wait one."

"Kilo 6 Alpha, over."

I pass the handset to the Lieutenant.

"Kilo 6 Actual. Why aren't you back yet? Over."

"Sir? Over."

"You are supposed to be back here before dark. It's almost dark, now. So get your ass back here Romeo Foxtrot November! Over."

Pause.

"Romeo Foxtrot November, Sir? Over."

"Right Fucking Now! COPY? Over."

"Copy. 6 Alpha out."

"You're damn right, copy. 6 Actual, out." Returns the handset to me.

"Thank you, Corporal. Sorry about the language."

"No biggie, Sir."

Kilo 6 Alpha returns in record time, Romeo Foxtrot November, before dark.

FNG Lieutenant

THE SKIPPER, BABY HUEY, approaches with another officer. A butter bar. Looks like a FNG.

Now what?

"Morton."

"Yes, Sir." Dare not call him Baby Huey to his face. Don't want to offend a 6'4" 250 pound ex-Berkeley cop.

"This is Lieutenant Barnes. He's the platoon leader of the new reinforcements."

"I see, Sir."

"He wants to run a sweep. I volunteered you to set up a blocking force. The Lieutenant will fill you in on the details."

"Yes, Sir."

Baby Huey slaps me on the back. "He's all yours, Lieutenant."

The Lieutenant hands me a map. A red grease pencil X on the map stands out.

"Corporal, this is where you will set up the blocking force." He taps a finger on the X. "Can you find that?"

With my head cocked to one side, I give him a stunned, quizzical look. *Gee-whiz, I think so. Dumb shit.*

He gets it, nods, then continues, "At zero-six hundred, you and one of my squads will head out the east gate. Me and the rest of the platoon will leave through the west gate at zero-six thirty. I don't care what route you take, just get there by zero-seven hundred. Our sweep will commence at zero-seven hundred. We will approach from the west. Understand?"

"Yes, Sir. Everyone know where we'll be? Grasshopper Nine, big guns at Con Thien, Camp Carroll, and Dong Ha? All are advised?"

"Yes, Corporal. Everyone is advised."

"Radio, Sir?"

"None available. I don't expect anything to happen. All I want to do is put on a show of force. You won't need a radio."

"Then, Sir, why do you need a blocking force?"

"Just in case."

"We should have a radio. Just in case, Sir."

"That will be all, Corporal. I'll have my men report to you this evening. You will handle the rest. Understand?"

"Yes, Sir." *FNG Lieutenant. Ain't good.*

0600

We start out the east gate. I walk point. I'm the only one I trust to get where we're going. Plus, these guys are way too green.

My boonie cover replaces my steel pot. No flak jacket. I carry ten magazines for my M16, and two bandoliers of ammo. A canteen of water on each hip. The squad carries the same. Except they wear their steel pots and flak jackets.

Double check my map, confirm our location.

Cam Lo, to our Northwest, looks isolated, sits far away, barely visible.

The ground in front of our position slopes down toward Route 9, to the east of the compound. Nothing but scrub brush between us and the road. A small stream or irrigation ditch, approximately 200 yards to our northeast, meanders through the brush, in large curves to wherever it ends. Only the high ridged banks of the ditch make it visible. The trickling pale brown water matches the color of the banks. It moves so slow, it hides from us, not visible. I know it's there. Been through it.

Son of a bitch! That's it! I'm out here because I'm familiar with the area. It doesn't matter, FNG Lieutenant, can't do a damn thing without a radio.

Position the men. Settle in. Hunker down. Check my watch. *0658, Good. We're early.*

No shade. Temperature rises.

0916

Unblocked, the sun glares down. Sears us through our clothes.

1035

Where are they? How long can it take? FNG Lieutenant get lost?

We begin to bake. The sun slow cooks us to the bone. Small talk stops. *Heat, dehydration.*

"Everybody, take your salt tabs."

They dig them out. Looks like a struggle. They pop the tabs into their mouths and wash them down with huge gulps of water from their canteens.

1145

We continue to bake in the blistering sun. No sweep approaches. Heat blisters well up under my moustache. The squad looks wrung out. I swirl my last swig of water in my mouth before I gulp it down.

FNG Lieutenant and his you don't need a radio.

"You. What's your name?"

"Lancaster."

"Gather up all the canteens. You see that gully down there, Lancaster? To our east."

He looks to where I point.

"Yeah. So?"

"So, Lancaster, there's water in that gully. Take the canteens there and fill them up. And get back here. On the double."

He starts gathering up the canteens.

Jeez, he's slower than the seven year itch in its fourteenth year.

"Move it, Lancaster."

He moves faster. *Not fast enough.*

"Jesus H. Christ, Lancaster! Move it!"

He shifts gears and moves with more urgency.

"You…."

"Carter."

"Carter. Give him a hand."

"Yes, Sir."

Carter gets up. Lancaster tosses him half the canteens. They hustle off, a beeline to the water. I watch them until they disappear into the gully. I scan the area. No movement around them. All still. No alarming sounds. No danger.

They reappear. Look loaded down, but move swiftly. In no time, they arrive. Distribute the canteens.

"Two halazone tabs in each canteen. Shake 'em up good."

Half hour later, enough time for the tabs to purify the water, I take a sip. Hot. Wet. Tastes like a water buffalo pissed in my mouth.

"Anyone got any Kool-Aid?" I look from one man to the next. Nothing but huh looks.

Lancaster shrugs his shoulders. "Kool-Aid?"

Guess that's a negative. "Makes the water taste better."

Dumb looks all around. Not until they take a sip do they get it. A few spit it out. The rest swallow hard.

"That's what for." I smile.

Looks and nods of understanding spread through the squad.

"It might taste shitty, but it's purified. It won't hurt you. It will help you get through the day."

Damn. These guys are newer than that FNG Lieutenant.

We all take big swigs, gulp them down. Drain my canteen. I suspect the others do, too.

It'll hold us. For a while.

1410

Still, nothing comes our way.

Enough.

"Lancaster. Carter."

Carter answers, "Yes, Sir?"

Lancaster nods.

"See the compound over there?" I point in the general direction. They strain to see it.

"It's just below the horizon.

"Look for the flag.

"White walls.

"Glares off roofs.

"Anything different from the brush."

"Oh, yeah. Got it."

"Good. Head there, stay east of it. At the road go west through the ville, on to the compound."

"Got it." Carter again.

Lancaster nods. Again. *What's with this guy? Can't talk?*

"We'll cover you. Anything happens we'll be there ASAP. At the compound, find out if we should stay out here. Or come in."

Both nod.

"How we gonna let you know? You got no radio."

Damn you, FNG Lieutenant.

"If stay, shoot off a red flare. Come in, green. Understand?"

"Yup."

True to form, Lancaster, the no talk nodder, nods.

What a pair.

"Well? Get going."

They load up their gear, much heavier now than 0630, then start out, in slow motion.

"Move it, goddam it!"

Their pace picks up.

The rest of the squad repositioned, my attention goes back to Carter and Lancaster.

They disappear, blend into the terrain. Hidden in the brush.

"Watch for flares, guys. Over there."

I point toward the compound.

They look.

Nods and thumbs up.

The nod squad. They're green. Sweaty. Drained. Still, holding up.

FNG Lieutenant.

1535

A flare rockets into the sky. Green burst.

"Let's go. We're heading in."

We saddle up. Rush back to the compound.

1653

Gear stored, I look for the stupid FNG Lieutenant. *Where are you, motherfucker?*

Baby Huey walks up to me. "He's gone."

"Where?"

"Doesn't matter. He's not here."

"Why not?"

"I advised him it might not be a good thing for him to be around when you got back. So, he left. I don't know where to. Sorry. This way, my friend, you stay out of trouble."

Stupid, Fucking Chicken Shit New Guy Lieutenant.

P-4

I FORGET REFUGEES are a major part of war. The relocation of the Montagnards or Bru brings the point home. P-HQ throws together a temporary CAP, P-4, to secure their safety until they can be relocated. It consists of one or two Marines from other PAPA CAPs. We run ambushes, walk patrols with the Montagnards, interact with them, and provide some medical care with our Corpsman.

All I know is they are refugees from Khe Sanh, relocating to Dóc Kình. The temporary ville and P-4 sit north of Camp Carroll on the junction of Route 9 and a small dirt road that runs south through some hills, skirts Camp Carroll, and ends in the valley where Dóc Kình sits.

A Vietnamese platoon joins us and the Montagnards, completes P-4. Vietnamese and Montagnards working together, being around each other, is not a good situation. They do not get along. They do not like each other. The Vietnamese consider the Montagnards inferior, second-class citizens. Our presence prevents problems between them.

We keep them as separated from each other as best we can. Ambushes and patrols are run with one faction or the other. Never both. The Montagnards are peaceful and friendly around us. Full of the joy of life, but with a cautious eye on the Vietnamese and the war. They are definitely in our corner. No ifs, ands, or buts. And no unlesses.

I am fond of them. The children are the best, the most interesting, the most innocent. Life in the village and our compound is non-eventful. All is calm. All is quiet. Everyone gets along. No issues. Almost as if we live in an oasis that cannot be touched by the war that continues all around us.

Ambushed

"ARE YOU SURE they know we'll pass in front of them around twenty-two forty-five or twenty-three hundred?"

"Trung Si Trang says he told them. Not to worry."

Not to worry? Montagnards moving past Vietnamese? At night? Lots to worry.

2245

"All set, Joe?"

"Always. Let's get going."

"Hang on. Remember, there's that RF ambush set up on the edge of the ville."

"They know we're coming, right?"

"That's what I'm told."

"No sweat then. Let's just go."

"Marsailles? Got enough ammo for the 60?"

"All I can carry. Enough."

A machine-gunner for Tail-End Charlie? Jeez. He wanted it.

"Get the Bru and form up."

2250

Amedeo leads four Bru, followed by me and Lefeve with the radio, four more Bru, and Marsailles, out the gate.

We enter the RF's ambush kill zone—THUNK.

Who the fuck fired the 81?

"Down. Down." I whisper-shout as loud as I dare.

The illum round bursts bright over us, lights us up like a spotlight. Halfway down to the deck, the RFs open fire on us. Purr of automatic gun fire sounds distant, but isn't.

"Hold your fire. Hold your fire. Marsailles do not fire."

Tracers whiz over us. I flatten out so much, I feel I am the thinnest I have ever been or will be in my life. Every red-glowing round seems it will find its mark, my head. I can barely breathe.

"Papa 4, Papa 4 Alpha. That's us they're firing at, goddam it. Tell them cease fire. Over."

"Nice going, Lefeve."

Firing stops, no more tracers. Quiet.

Take a breath, Tom.

"Anyone hit? Hurt?"

"Twisted my knee." Only Amedeo answers.

"Can you walk?"

"Barely."

"Just turn around. Marsailles will take us back."

"Okay. Let's go."

"Marsailles?"

"Ready."

"Move out."

No one fesses up. Nor does anyone know who fires the 81.

Probably fucking Trang or one of his boys. I find out, he's a dead motherfucker.

Dinner with the Chief

ONE OF THE official duties of a CAP unit is dinner with the Village Chief and his family. Maintains good relations between the villagers and us. My turn to dine with the Chief comes up.

My fire team, our interpreter, and I sit round the table with the Village Chief, his wife, and their daughter.

He, a wizened man of about 40, considered a fierce warrior by his people.

Her, not a bad looking lady. Until she smiles. Her teeth stained black from chewing betel nut. Otherwise, it is a good smile.

The daughter, a cute 15 or 16-year-old, a developing young woman with dark skin and eyes, long straight black hair and a smile with the first hints of developing a smile to match her mother's.

Turns out the dinner is for a special reason. The Village Chief offers his daughter to me for marriage. I have no idea why. To maintain good relationships? To provide his daughter a better life in America?

No thanks. I'll pass. How do I turn down the offer without offending the Village Chief and his wife, and not hurt the girl?

Through our interpreter, I explain I am honored, but I am happily married. *Maybe.*

Disappointed, the family apologizes for making the offer and hope I am not offended.

Offended? No way!

I accept the apology. Explain I am not offended, but honored.

Another bullet, one aimed at me, dodged.

Good relations maintained. All is good. Nothing to worry about.

Trotting

SARGE SHAKES ME awake. "Get up, Morton. You've slept in long enough."

"I don't think so, Sarge."

"It's zero-seven hundred. Get up." *What a hard ass.*

"Okay. Okay."

"How'd it go last night?"

I sit up on the edge of my cot. "Not much to talk about. Had dinner with the Chief and his family. He tried to marry off his daughter to me."

"You're shitting me."

"I wouldn't do that."

"I know. I'm your favorite turd. Ha. Ha. Last time I heard that, I laughed so hard, I almost fell off my dinosaur."

We stare and smile at each other for a couple of seconds.

Sarge breaks the silence. "Well?"

"Well what?"

"How'd you handle the daughter-marriage thing? Did you accept?" A grin replaces his smile.

"Yeah. Right." Shake my head, "No. I respectfully and diplomatically declined."

"You? Respectfully? Diplomatically?"

"Uh-huh. I'm capable of showing respect and using diplomacy. It's hard for me, but I'm capable." *I've been at this civic action thing longer than you.*

"So, how'd you, respectfully and diplomatically, decline?"

"I thanked them for the offer. Told him I had a wife back in the World."

"They handle it okay?"

"Yeah. Apologetic as all get out. I told them I was honored they chose me for their daughter."

"All is well?"

"Yeah. All is well."

"Good."

I climb out of my cot. Stomach a little queasy.

A new day dawns in the Nam, my stomach still a little uneasy. First order of business, a dump.

The one-hole shitter smells bad. The heat makes it worse. As soon as I sit, all kinds of crap comes flying out, splashes, with a goosh into the diesel fuel in the half of a fifty-five gallon drum.

No shit? No, lots of shit.

I feel better. Stomach feels settled.

The day drags by.

Nausea wakes me up in the middle of the night. I puke into my steel pot, fill it. The same with my shaving bowl.

"Goddammit, that stinks. Get that shit the fuck outta here."

Rinse water in my mouth prevents me from replying with a smart ass retort. I have no place to spit out the vomit-tainted water. Off to the shitter to empty my steel pot and shaving bowl. Spit out the water along the way.

Everything cleaned up, I plop onto my cot.

Better. Not quite right. But better.

The bustling about by my tent mates wakes me up.

Jeez, I just went to sleep.

I sit up and swing my legs over the edge of my cot. *Whoa.*

My hands on the edge of the cot steady me. The dizziness goes away.

I stand up. Stomach growls, flip-flops. *What the fuck?*

Barely to the shitter in time, my trousers thrown down around my ankles. I sit. One long squirt hits the bottom, sounds like water jetted from a firehose into a swimming pool.

Great. The shits.

Nothing remains to explode out of me. I pull myself up. *Damn!* Dizzy again, I throw my hands out to the walls. *Steady.*

Braced with hands, arms, and walls, my balance returns. My stomach gurgles, nonstop, all the way back to the tent.

My head hurts. I am tired. Know I should lay down, I look to Sergeant Wilson. *Gotta let him know.*

Sarge, at the far end of the tent, busies himself cleaning his 45.

"Sarge."

"What?"

"I'm not feeling so good. Headache, squirrelly stomach, and the shits. I'm gonna lay down for a bit."

"Have Doc check you out. Whatever he says is what you'll do."

"Fine." *Your cup runneth over with concern.*

Off to Doc's tent.

A quick, awkward, cheeks-clenched jog to the shitter interrupts my search for Doc. I'm anxious to get on the wooden seat with the ass-size hole in the middle.

Hurry, hurry, hurry.

Just in time, this jaunt ends at its destination.

Cleaned up, I stumble out of the shitter, get my bearings, regain my balance. Then, make my way to Doc's tent.

"Doc?"

"Yeah?" Turns to me, leans back. "You don't look so good. You okay?"

"No. Got the shits, upset stomach, headache, dizzy, weak, tired. Ache all over."

He checks my temperature.

"One hundred point two. Probably just a little bug is all or something you ate didn't agree with you."

From his shelves of medical supplies, he pulls out two bottles.

"Here. Take these."

He shakes out a couple of tablets from one bottle into my hand.

"Wash them down with this."

The cup he hands me is full of white liquid from the other bottle. *Milk of Magnesia?*

After tossing the tablets into my mouth, I throw back the liquid chalk like a tequila shot.

One big gulp. Everything seeps down my throat. Rumbles in my stomach lessen. Then, are gone. *Not bad.*

"Take the day off. Hit the sack. Get some rest."

"Piece of cake, Doc."

"I'll let Sarge know. If things don't get better, your symptoms persist, or diarrhea continues, come see me."

"Will do. Thanks, Doc."

"No problem." He goes back to whatever he was doing before I got here.

I shuffle back to my tent. When I flop onto my cot, my stomach rumbles. *Stop it.* It does. *Good.*

I sink deeper into my cot.

Before I fall asleep, Sarge appears. Stands over me.

"Doc told me."

Sympathy is not a part of his demeanor.

All I'm able to do is look up at him.

"How about something to eat?" He smirks.

Very funny.

Nausea hits me. With a hard swallow, it goes away. "No, thanks." A few sips of water moisten my dry mouth. I feel a little better. Comfortable on my cot. Doc's remedies do their jobs. A deep breath. I fall asleep.

I awake. Weak and tired, I sit up onto the edge of my cot. It is dark.

Not dizzy, I take a deep breath. I am thirsty.

Grab my canteen. Couple of swigs. The water cascades down my throat. Splashes into my stomach.

Hunger makes its presence felt.

The water sloshes around in my stomach as I cross the tent to our supply of C-Rations. The first one I grab is Chopped Ham and Eggs. Beats Ham and Motherfuckers.

Eat. Back to my cot.

The Chopped Ham and Eggs wastes no time shooting through me.

Finally, sleep.

Propped up on one elbow, I look around the tent. "Lee."

A grunt.

"Help me up."

"Help yourself up."

"No, really. I need your help."

Disgruntled, he walks over, looks down at me. His annoyed look flashes into one of shock.

"Holy crap! You look like shit. I'm getting Doc." He darts out the tent.

"What's wrong?" Doc sits on the edge of my cot.

"I can't get up. I feel exhausted, weak, everything hurts, insides feel like goo."

"When's the last time you took a leak or crapped?" His hand on my forehead.

"Don't remember."

"Okay. Take it easy. We gotta get you to Delta Med." *That bad?*

"I'll call HQ. Get transportation. Be right back."

Close my eyes, feel as if my body dissolves into my cot.

"They're on their way." Doc puts his arm under my arm, raises me into a sitting position.

"Take a sip." Doc lifts a cup of water to my mouth. The few sips I take don't feel as if they make it to my stomach.

Doc eases me back down. The water ebbs and flows between my stomach and mouth.

After forever, Smitty arrives with the PC. He and Doc carry me to the truck. Load me into the back. Doc stays with me. Smitty gets into the driver's seat, starts and revs the engine.

We depart for Delta Med. The bumps on the road rattle my bones, not anything else. There is nothing inside me to jostle. Complete emptiness.

The PC stops.

"We're here." While Doc lifts me up, Smitty hops out of the truck, scurries around to help him get me to the door of Delta Med. Corpsmen meet us there. They ease me onto a stretcher.

Doc mumbles something to them.

"We'll get him to a doctor right away."

The noise inside is loud, but gentle. Everyone moves about with purpose, in earnest. Doctors and Corpsmen labor at operating tables. Looks like a busy day.

A short exam and interrogation, the doctor pronounces his diagnosis.

"Dysentery." As he turns to a cabinet, "Severely dehydrated."

Pulls out three medicine bottles, "Probably something you ate." *Mystery meat at Village Chief dinner?*

One bottle has clear fluid in it. Another, Milk of Magnesia. The third, pint sized, is empty.

The doctor pours Milk of Magnesia into the empty bottle, fills it halfway.

"I'm making what I like to call my Dysentery Cocktail."

Adds the clear liquid to fill the bottle, "It's half this, paregoric acid. And half Milk of Magnesia."

The cap secure on the bottle of his special concoction, he vigorously shakes it. Finished, he hands it to me.

"Drink half right now. Chug it."

Down it goes. Gags me.

He takes the bottle. Pours more of those two godawful ingredients into it. Shakes it.

Hands it back to me.

"Every time you feel like you have to go, shake this up, take a swig of it, like from a bottle of booze. You should feel a lot better in a day or so."

A day or so? Already, I feel like my ass is as watertight as a frog's.

"We'll keep you here for a few hours. Get some fluids in you."

He turns to the Corpsman next to him. "Franks, get two IVs going."

"A double dose?"

"Yes. Then, put him against a wall, out of the way."

Franks does what he's told. Directs two other Corpsmen to put me on a stretcher.

I end up alongside a wall, out of the way, with an IV in each arm. A clear fluid finds its way from bottles hanging on some sort of wire stand, down a tube, through needles in my arms into my veins.

As I doze, I hear all that is going on around me.

"Poor guy. Two IVs."

"Whatever happened to him must've been pretty bad."

All I got's the shits, goddammit. I'll be okay. A lot of the guys in here won't be.

In The Ville

A COMBAT ZONE heightens awareness and senses. When I hear mortars, artillery, rockets fire off in the distance, I know if they are coming my way.

I hear the sound of mortars firing. They are headed in my direction. I gather up my gear and start for the bunkers. Everyone does. We hear the explosions of the 61 mm mortar shells.

"Shit! Those hit the ville!"

We run toward the explosions. It doesn't appear bad. A few huts hit, damage minimal. And, it is quiet. The smoke smells of cordite and dirt of a freshly plowed field, drifts languidly through the area.

Slowly, it starts. Screams, sobs. Sergeant Cook and I run into a slightly damaged hut, drawn in by the screams. Screams of children.

We find three little girls, the oldest about twelve years old. All three scream uncontrollably, scared out of their minds. They are on their knees around what appears to be a woman. But the woman seems small, smaller than she should be.

When we get to her and the children, we see why. Only shreds of her pant legs remain where her legs should be. She is drenched in blood. Her head turns side to side, looks from child to child. The children's faces, wet with tears, contort in horror. They are afraid to touch her. Blood is spattered on them, but they are not wounded.

We rush to help the woman. To get to her wounds, we tear away what remains of her clothes. Numerous shrapnel wounds dot her head, arms, and abdomen. Blood spurts from where her legs once were.

She looks at us, one at a time, not really seeing us. All goes quiet, so it seems, as we try to stop the bleeding where her legs had been. There is no place to tie a tourniquet. Finding the artery is unsuccessful. As the blood flow slows, so do her head and arm movements.

Then, she is still. Check her eyes. Nothing. For her, it is over. Sarge starts CPR. I don't know what else to do. There is nothing more I can do. Sit, watch as he tries to revive her. I know she is dead. Her children know. Finally, in a daze, so does Sarge. It is quiet. I feel helpless, responsible, and vengeful.

Suddenly, I hear the children again. All the other sounds in the ville become audible as well. The girls' sobs become more mournful and heartbreaking.

"Sarge. Sarge! Dan!"

He looks at me. His eyes angry-red, his face wet from sweat. And tears.

"I fucking hate those goddam bastards! They try but can't zero in on us. And these people end up paying for it."

There is nothing more we can do. Check the rest of the ville. Our guys take care of the wounded. Call in Medevac choppers.

The wounded are flown to Delta Med in Dong Ha.

The villagers tend to the dead and the children.

Doc Clap

Doc Emerson scans the group.

"Ross and Perez are due back from Thailand. I'll be on R & R when they get back. They'll probably have the clap. Who wants to learn how to give injections?"

I raise my hand. "I already know how. Doc Young taught me when we were at Papa 5."

"You sure?"

"Yeah."

"You don't mind shooting their asses full of penicillin?"

"Nope. Done it before."

He shows me where he stores needles, syringes, and the penicillin.

Two days after Doc leaves for Hawaii, Ross and Perez return from their R & R. Two happy, sated guys, they are.

"Where's Doc?" They sound alarmed.

"R & R. Hawaii. Why?"

I know why.

"We got the clap."

"I can take care of that." I smile.

"You? No thanks."

"It's a sharp needle in the ass and no mention on your medical record. Or a burning dick till Doc gets back. Which will it be?"

"You're no Corpsman. We'll wait for Doc."

"Suit yourselves." *You'll be back.*

Perez wakes me up.

"Okay, Morton. Let's do it."

Ross is right behind him.

"Me, too."

Three days, I shoot them up.

They are pain free and happy now.

They call me, "Doc Clap."

Last Days

THREE DAYS, I di Hao Ky. From my perch atop the comm bunker, I gaze across Route 9, over the ville, to the Cua Viet River. Lean back in my beach chair, radio at my side, feel cocky. I wear the swim trunks I bought while on R & R, boonie cover, and jungle boots. I am one salty son of a bitch.

Hao Ky, land of round-eyed women, family and friends, and no one shooting at me. No 120° summer days, no monsoon season with sheets of rain so thick I can't see my hand in front of my face, and only one more year in The Crotch.

Unbelievable I survive this year, too many close calls, too much death and destruction, friends and beaucoup dong bao killed. All a waste and nothing changes. The war continues. Ahh, we will win, eventually. Not because of me. I only help it linger on.

Dust from the direction of Dong Ha, comes straight down Route 9, in my direction.

Must be Matson on his weekly supply run. He first stops here which gives us the pick of the supplies.

I pick up the handset. Check off the net. Climb down off the bunker and amble down the slope to the road to liberate whatever delectable items are on Matson's three-quarter ton PC, especially the beer.

BOOM!

An explosion from the ville, a cloud of dust and smoke billows into the air.

I race through the gate, rush toward the scene. Behind me I hear the guys gather their gear, scramble in the same direction.

Matson turns the PC to the ville. Brodies to a stop. Jumps out. Hurries to the ville, me close behind.

No sound. Yet. All quiet. Slowly, the screams, shouts, laments and cries start. There must be dead or wounded, probably both.

A woman stumbles out to us, a small child in her arms.

Dammit! Another dead kid. The kid moves. *Yes!*

Muddied tears crawl down the woman's face.

Matson rushes to her. Lifts the baby from her arms. Hands it to me.

"Let's go."

Dart to the PC. Slide in.

Matson gets in. Hits the gas. We fishtail a U-turn. Race to Dong Ha and Delta Med.

I look down at the baby. A boy. His sad big brown eyes focus on me. He appears to be fine, no tears, no nothing, just breathes. I scan his torso. See it, the reason for our mad dash down Route 9. A gash in his abdomen exposes a large portion of his intestines, not enough to hang out, but enough to bulge through the belly skin. No emotion from the kid.

An MP stops us at the gate of Dong Ha Marine Combat Base. He looks in. "You can't bring a kid in here." He looks closer, sees the problem. "Holy shit! Go! Go! Go!"

Matson floors it. Dirt and dust fly up into the air.

At Delta Med, Matson opens the door for me. I hurry into the hospital. Corpsmen rush up, take the baby.

"We got it from here."

That's what we're supposed to do.

A good ending to a bad year.

Back into the PC. Return to the comm bunker.

Scrutinize what I see before me. Shadows creep eastward. Route 9 devoid of traffic. Vegetation grows dark as the light of day retreats. River motionless. The ville quiet. A quiet born of the day's events.

Three days, I di Hao Ky.

Home

Going

CONTINENTAL AIRLINES BECOMES my favorite airline the moment we lift off the runway at Danang Airport, heading to the World. All us Marines cheer. The stewardesses are gorgeous round eyes, with short skirts and big tits.

One walks down the aisle past me. Palm trees in a breeze come to mind. A few rows down, she bends over to talk to a Marine. The view exhilarates.

He gets an eye full, too. Of cleavage.

The flight is anything but restful. Excitement, anticipation, rowdiness rule supreme.

0830

Touch down in Okinawa. Wild cheers. After processing, the pogues point us to the E-Club and the NCO Club.

"They opened early just for you guys."

A stampede to the clubs.

First arrivals grab stools at the bar. I secure a spot at the corner of the L-shape bar.

Choices of beverages are boundless.

What to have. What to have.

I can't decide. No one can.

"Sloe gin fizz!" Someone shouts. It doesn't sound manly. Sounds exotic, not manly.

Everyone orders sloe gin fizzes.

Cute looking drink, tastes a bit on the wimpy side. I can drink these all day long. Throw one back. Some do the same. Some sip. Some just taste.

Lunchtime arrives. Hamburgers, BLTs, bacon and eggs, steak sandwiches, fries, you name it, it is ordered and served right here at the bar.

Sloe gin fizzes continue.

Late afternoon. "I gotta piss!" A guy turns on his barstool, stands, and falls flat on his face, out cold.

A collective, "Whoa!"

We hug the bar and laugh. Two employees tend to our fallen comrade.

More sloe gin fizzes.

From then on, whenever one of us goes to the head, it's hold onto the bar, slide off the stool, use the stool as a brace to steady yourself and turn, head for the head, use whatever means of support available to and from. Upon return, use the bar for support to pull up onto the barstool.

More sloe gin fizzes.

Dinner consists of whatever anyone wants. They have it all.

After dinner, sloe gin fizzes flow again.

"Hey! Morton!"

Turn toward the voice, I come face-to-face with Alshback.

"What the hell?"

We exchange pleasantries, tell a few stories of the past year.

"Come on. Let's go into town."

"Can't. We're restricted to base. No liberty card."

A grin splashes across his face. "You know what I've been doing for the last year here in Okinawa?"

"Not a clue."

"Signing liberty cards for the Major."

"Reeeeeealy?"

"Uh-huh. 10 bucks gets you one."

"Oooh-kay."

Alshback returns in an hour with liberty cards for me and six others.

"Hi ho, hi ho. It's off to town we go." *Wish I said that.*

End of sloe gin fizz day.

Night one of Drink and Debauchery begins.

The next three days are roll calls at 0700, processing, then base liberty at 1600. Except for those of us with liberty cards, it's another night of D and D.

Then, at last, board a Continental flight for home.

Hours pass.

The pilot announces, "Gentlemen, to the left is Seattle, the World."

Cheers as the right side passengers pile to the left side to peer out the windows. It is a miracle we don't go into a left wing dive.

We land in Seattle, followed by San Francisco, then, Marine Corps Air Base, El Toro, California.

Welcome

WE LAND AT El Toro in the afternoon. We process out, get on a Navy bus to the Greyhound Depot in Santa Ana. On the way, we come across some war protesters. All have long hair. A Gunnery Sergeant suggests we stop the bus, cut the hair off all the protesters, make a mattress from the hair, and send it to some Marine in the Nam.

We don't.

I catch a Greyhound bus to San Diego, arrive in the early evening. A cab takes me to my mother-in-law's house, where Diane stays. It is hard to find. At 2330, I ring the doorbell.

Joy half fills me. The other half, apprehension.

Her mother answers the door. "Oh, my God."

Diane comes up behind her. She looks shocked. It takes a few seconds for her to come to me. We hug then kiss, once.

Her mom breaks the awkward moment, "Well, come on in. Beer?"

"Yes, thank you, ma'am."

"Me, too, Mom."

Some chitchat fills the time it takes me to guzzle my beer.

"Well, you two will want to spend some time alone. Have some fun."

She hands me some money and her car keys.

"Go get a motel. I'll see you in the morning. For breakfast?"

"Yeah, sure, Mom."

Bitchin.

We check into a motel and do what young couples do after a long separation.

In the morning, she says she has morning sickness.

My mind tells me the timing is not quite right. Something's wrong. I figure she is pregnant and I had nothing to do with it. The looks we lock onto each other say what needs to be said. I know. She knows I know. Time to cut myself loose from this bad situation.

Toss her the car keys.

"Go home to your mother. We're done."

She takes them and leaves.

The rest of the day I spend at the E-Club at MCRD, drinking cheap beer. When night falls, I call Dad. He is happy I'm home in one piece.

"Does your mother know you're back?"

"No."

"Better call her, son. She's worried sick about you. Go see her. We can get together later."

Another cab ride to my next stop, Mom's. This house is easy to find. I know where it is.

I ring the doorbell, not sure what to expect. Some genuine happiness would be nice.

Candy answers the door.

"Tommy! Mom! It's Tommy! It's Tommy!" *How can she have tears in her eyes and grin at the same time?*

Mom comes out from her bedroom. She looks unsure.

When I step through the door, she is sure, runs to me, throws her arms around my neck and buries her face in my chest, sobs, "Tommy. Tommy."

Tears not good for the uniform.

Who gives a shit?

I push her back and kiss her forehead.

"You was expectin' someone else?"

"Oh, Tommy!" She slaps my arm, dabs her eyes. "Welcome home."

Hug Candy. Her eyes are dry and red, but the grin remains.

"Yeah, welcome home, big brother."

"Thanks. Good to be home. Where's Val?"

"She has her own apartment. Come on. We'll go over. She'll be glad to see you and there's someone she wants you to meet."

Oh, wonderful. She got married.

Mom has me stand back as she rings the doorbell. Val answers the door in her bathrobe.

"Mom. It's after midnight. What are you doing here?"

"Someone to see you."

Mom pulls me forward, and pushes me through the doorway.

Val screams. "Tommy! Oh my God!"

"I hope you didn't wake up the neighborhood."

"I don't care. You're home."

She gathers me into a big sisterly hug. She cries.

Uniform's takin' a beatin'.

I don't a shit.

"Welcome home, Tommy. Come here. Come here. I want you to meet someone."

She grabs my hand, and leads me to what I guess is the bedroom.

She's going to wake up her husband? So I can meet him? While he's still in bed?

"Valerie, are you crazy?"

"No." A thin smile shows she is up to something.

In the bedroom, she flicks on a small lamp.

Yes, let's blind the poor guy.

She pulls me to a corner of the room. I see it. A baby crib.

"Tommy, this is your nephew, Sean-Paul."

"What? How come you didn't let me know?"

"We didn't want to upset you or worry you. You had enough on your mind."

"Yeah, I guess. Still."

We go out to the living room.

"How old is he?"

"Four months. Where's Diane? Have you seen her yet?"

"Yeah, she had morning sickness after our first night."

Val tee-hees.

Mom, "Uh-huh."

"What?"

"Never mind."

"I told her we're done."

"Good for you."

"I always wondered what you saw in ol' thunder thighs."

"Mom!"

"Sorry."

We chit-chat for an hour. Mom goes home. I crash on Val's couch.

My uniform is a mess. In the morning, I'll put on some civvies. And, have breakfast with my first nephew.

This welcome home is better.

I fuss with Sean-Paul. Val makes me a great breakfast. My first home-cooked meal in over a year. As I eat, she prepares his bottle. I sop up the last of the yolk with the final scrap of toast, and pop it into my mouth, then reach for my nephew. Val hands him to me, then the bottle. I feed the little guy.

Talk about a sweet first real meal back in the world, could not be much better than this.

"I called Barbara."

"Reynolds?"

"Yes. She's on her way over."

"Why?"

"You know. You promised."

"She's going to hold me to that?"

"Yup."

"Do I really have to keep it?"

"Well, yeah. What's the matter, Tommy? Your alligator mouth catch up with your hummingbird ass? You know how she feels."

"I know how she felt, once, a long time ago, when you two were freshmen and I was a senior. She still feels that way?" *I don't need this.*

"Why do you think she's on her way over? I told her you're single again."

"Thanks." *I wish I hadn't promised her I'd take her out when she turned 18, if I was single. How bad could it be? One date?*

After breakfast, I call Grandma.

"Hi, Grandma. Guess who's home."

"Ay dios mio, mijito." Her voice cracks. She clears her throat. "How long have you been here?"

"I got in night before last."

"When do I get to see you?"

"Tomorrow for lunch?"

"Si. What would you like me to make?"

"Lemon meringue pie and milk from Miller's Dairy in the glass bottle."

"Okay. Mañana. Welcome home, mijo."

"Thanks, Grandma. Mañana."

Tomorrow comes. I gobble up the whole pie. Gulp the ice cold half-gallon of milk, straight from the bottle.

In the evening, Dad takes me out to dinner at the Chiefs' Club on the Coronado Amphibious Base.

"Good to have you home, son. I'm glad you made it home safe. Where were you wounded?"

"Side of my face, head."

"It doesn't show."

"Nothing to show."

"I thought I told you to keep your head down, Jarhead."

"I did, squid. That's why I'm still here, Dad."

He looks at me from across the table for a second before he smiles a grateful smile.

"Let's order."

It is good to be home.

1969
Final Year

Visit at the PX

DOWN THE AISLE I see a familiar figure.

"Secret Squirrel." *Only one person in the world will respond.*

The figure turns its head. The smile turns into a grin. *There's that chipped front tooth. It is him.*

"Super Skate."

Long strides to each other. Handshake. Hug. Slaps on backs.

"Damn, I thought you were dead. I went by your unit. They said you got shot up bad. I wrote you a few times. Got no answer."

"Never got them. They moved me from Delta Med to the Repose, to Japan, to San Diego, to Great Lakes Naval Hospital. One place to another. So fast, I guess your letters couldn't catch up. Stayed in Great Lakes hospital. They thought it good to be close to my family while I recovered."

"Oh, yeah. Minnie-soooota."

He nods his head, his wry smile appears. "I was in there for a little over four months. Then, they let me go home for six weeks to finish healing. Then, I got orders to come back here. It was so good being home, I didn't want to go back just then. Wasn't ready. They said I was. So, I took 30 days leave. And now, here I am. Getting short."

"I'm happy as a pig in shit that you didn't buy the farm."

"You think you are? I'm the happiest of all. Well, maybe next to my mom."

He looks deadly serious. We laugh nervous laughs. They fade out.

I break the quiet. "Well?"

"Well? What happened in Nam?"

My lone slow nod triggers his deep breath sigh. His grin looks sheepish.

"I got shot in the ass."

Too funny. Maybe not that funny.

"I know what you're thinking. Funny, huh?" His normal grin returns.

"Yeah. Thinking funny. I know it's not. Sorry."

"That's okay. It's funny now. Not when I was being extracted under fire."

Damn.

"I was the last one hoisted up. Just as I was being pulled aboard, WHAP. I get this sharp burning feeling in my ass. That's the last thing I remember till I woke up in some hospital in Japan."

"What a bummer."

"Some lucky NVA son of a bitch on the ground shot me in the ass. The round ripped from my left ass cheek all the way up across my back to my right shoulder."

"Not good."

"Right. But, Corpsmen and doctors all took good care of me." He nods, face expressionless.

"You okay?"

Another sigh. "I guess. Got a nifty scar out of it. My bodybuilding contests days are over, though."

Now, that's funny. We chuckle.

"It got infected. They had to cut me open from where the round went in to where it lodged. The infection got so bad, it took a long time before they could close me back up."

"Long time before they could close it?"

"They left it open, so they could clean it out every day. Spent most of my time on my stomach. Some on my side."

"I couldn't do that."

"You do what you gotta do. Anyway, here I am. All in one piece with an impressive as hell scar." He grins again. I smile with several nods.

"I gotta get back."

"Me, too."

"Later at the E-Club for a few brewskis and bullshitting?"

"Agreed."

Out the door. Go our separate ways, to finish another day in the Big Green Machine.

Memorial Service

FORGE A BOY into a man, an individual physically and mentally tough with confident self-reliance to apply skills into a team effort. Mold him into a United States Marine.

To do this, Drill Instructors tear you down, build you back up, mold you, convince you all is possible and you can do whatever they say you can. They instill trust and confidence in you and your fellow Marines. They create a self-reliant member of a team that has faith in itself, believes in team work. Work together — GUNG HO! They build a can-do-will-do team foundation on which each Marine stands.

At the end of boot camp, you believe in yourself, have faith in others. You are a United States Marine.

Drill Instructors accomplish this because first you fear them. Then, you trust them. And love them. Revere them. All things are possible if a Drill Instructor tells you so.

The news shakes me through and through. The shock weighs heavy on me. I must go.

I drive from Camp Pendleton to MCRD on autopilot.

Sounds of weeping seep into my ears when I enter the chapel. It is his widow. Swedish good looking blond. Just like him. But she is not him. She is here. He is not.

A pew in the rear invites me to rest. Numbed by everything, I sit.

I stare off into space. See nothing. Noise, music, voices drift up, echo off the high ceiling. Voices say....I don't know what. Music incomprehensible. Noise of nothingness.

Deafeningly unclear, a mass of silent cacophony.

He was invincible, indestructible. How could he be dead?

KIA in Viet Nam.

I experienced combat. I understand no one is invincible, indestructible, not even my revered Senior Drill Instructor, Sergeant Peters.

I salute you.

I thank you.

You taught me how to survive.

And live.

Corporal of the Guard

A FAVORITE OF the company commander I am not. It seems the Lieutenant does not like anybody. He might not be happy he is called up from the reserves.

To show he is in command, he assigns me to Corporal of the Guard duty. Duty away from his command, out of his unit. Out of his hair. This duty must be boring, stuck on base every day, every night, and every weekend. He's got me. I'll be stuck on base until I get out of the Corps. Four long months. Shitty duty.

Corporal of the Guard shifts are twenty-four hours on, twenty-four hours off. My liberty card stays in my possession at all times. When not on duty, I can go off base, to the beach, get in some surfing time. I can do what I want and go where I want.

The platoon, fresh from boot camp, is squared away. Eager to please.

1600

I form the platoon on the parade ground and make sure all are present and accounted for. The OD comes out from his office.

"Platoon, ten-hut!"

They snap to attention.

The OD strides up to me.

I salute. "Good afternoon, Sir."

Returning my salute, "Good afternoon, Corporal. Report."

"All present and accounted for, Sir."

"Very well. Carry on."

"Aye-Aye, Sir."

I salute. He returns it, does an about-face, disappears into his office.

March the platoon to the Mess Hall for evening chow. We eat. Then, back to the barracks.

Twenty minutes later, I conduct a rifle and personnel inspection of the first squad.

They fall out on to the road outside the office. These just-out-of-boot-camp Marines look sharp. Razor creased uniforms. Spit shined shoes. Standing tall. A-J squared away.

The squad leader calls them to attention.

The inspection begins.

It goes well until one man's rifle hits the underside of the bill of my cover as he performs his inspection arms. It flips off my head. Lands in the dirt.

He looks petrified. He does not know what to do. This is not addressed in boot camp. He steps to pick it up. Onto my right foot. Scuffs the spit shine.

The look of horror on his face makes me want to laugh. I do not, except on the inside. This is a deadly serious situation to him. He comes back to inspection arms.

"Sir, I …." He goes stone-faced.

"Yes?"

"Sir. Sorry. Sir."

I bend over to pick up my cover. *Don't let him see my smile.*

Back up and face-to-face with him once again.

I finish the inspection. Not another word is spoken.

After his shift, that Marine visits me at the Corporal of the Guard desk.

"Sir, I'm real sorry about your cover and your shoe, Sir."

"I'm not an officer and I'm not your father. Do not call me Sir. You may address me as Corporal or Corporal Morton.'

"Yes, Corporal. I'll re-shine them, Sir."

He notices my head tilt.

"I mean, Corporal."

"Don't worry about it. It's no big deal. I already did it."

He looks relieved.

Out on the parade ground waiting for the OD. An officer I recognize steps from the OD's office. It is a CO I had in Viet Nam, the Captain we affectionately called Baby Huey.

He approaches.

"Platoon, ten-hut!"

I salute.

"Good afternoon, Baby Huey."

With a smile, returns my salute, "Hey, Mort. Report."

"All present and accounted for, Skipper."

"Good. Take them to chow. After posting, report to my office, in civvies."

"Aye, Sir."

We exchange salutes, he does an about-face, and returns to his office.

I report to his office as ordered, in civvies.

The Skipper, in civvies, sits at his desk.

"All your guys out there okay?"

"Yes, Sir."

"Good. We're going to the O-Club for a drink."

"Ah, Sir...."

"As of now you are Lieutenant Morton."

"I like that!"

"Don't get used to it, Corporal."

We laugh.

At the Corporal of the Guard desk, just before midnight, a group of my troops returns from their Cinderella Liberty. They are excited about something. They are not old enough to buy booze. So, they can't be drunk.

"Corporal, the new Playboy's out!" They are old enough to buy Playboy.

"The Playmate of the Month is out-fucking-standing!"

"She's built like a brick shit house!"

"Solid!"

"You got my attention. Let's see her."

They show me the centerfold. I cannot believe my eyes. "That's Lorrie Menconi!"

"You know her?"

"I did once."

"Bullshit!"

Looking over and around each other, they take another look at her.

"No bullshit. I'm from San Diego. She's from San Diego. Check it out."

Doesn't take them long.

"No shit!"

"Do you know her now?"

"Wish I did. I knew her in the seventh or eighth grade. I'd go swimming at the La Mesa Pool. A little, skinny, flat-chested girl, in a little girl bikini chased me around the pool. Everywhere I went, there she was. Her name was Lorrie Menconi." Another glance at the centerfold. "She sure did fill out."

"Don't you wish she'd chase you now?"

"Wouldn't be much of a chase!"

We crack up.

Corporal of the Guard duty is good duty. I enjoy Corporal of the Guard duty. I come and go as I please. I am idolized by just-out-of-boot camp, Gung Ho Marines. Too good to be true.

The Lieutenant finds out just how good. He recalls me after thirty days of a ninety day assignment. Under his thumb. Again.

Shit.

Final Inspection

THE LIEUTENANT ASSIGNS me Training NCO duties.

Lots of work, schedule classes and instructors, bring files up to date.

An upcoming IG inspection is foremost on the Lieutenant's mind. He wants a good inspection report. He harasses me about things other than the training needs and files.

"Sir, if you want these records to pass inspection, you must let me do my job. There's too much that needs to be done for me to be distracted by other things."

"I see." Something about that I see.

"Will I be standing the rifle and personnel inspection, Sir?"

"No. You will stand by in your office."

"Yes, Sir."

In the training office, I await the IG. I will be here all day during the inspection. I relax in my chair behind my desk.

Corporal Slagle, the company clerk, pokes his head in, "The Lieutenant says for you to get up to the inspection."

"I don't think so. He told me I don't have to stand inspection."

"I just came from him. He says you do. Better hurry. Starts pretty soon."

Up from my chair, around my desk and out the door to the company office to see the Lieutenant.

"Sir, you told me I wouldn't have to stand inspection."

"I changed my mind, Corporal. Get to the armory, get your piece, and get up there."

218

Our eyes lock on each other. No flinches from either one of us.

"Aye-Aye, Sir."

Rush to the armory. Get my M14. Scamper to the inspection area.

I have not seen my rifle for months. It is dusty. Filthy. Check the bore. There's enough dirt down there to grow potatoes. *Fuck.*

I don't have time to go back to the barracks to clean it. It will have to stay this way.

The outside of my piece is no problem. I borrow Unger's brush and dust it off. It looks great on the outside. Perfect as long as no one looks down the barrel. If someone does, I am dead meat.

"Company! Ten- hut!"

We do.

"Dress, right, dress!"

We do.

"Parade rest!"

We do.

The inspection begins. I am in the middle of the third rank. The first two ranks do not fare well, lots of low voice reprimands. The third rank is not doing much better. The inspecting officer, a Full Bird Colonel, gets to the man to my right. Slagle to the right of the Colonel, faces me. The Lieutenant, on the other side of the Colonel. Slagle looks at me, blinks and shakes his head.

The guy next to me has a hard time. The Colonel, in a low voice, reads him the riot act for Irish pennants, lack of military knowledge and not doing a good inspection arms.

The Colonel moves to me. I see the Lieutenant out of the corner of my eye. He flashes a smirky smile.

I perform a perfect inspection arms.

"That's the best inspection arms I've seen all morning, Lieutenant."

The Lieutenant raises his eyes upward. Smirk disappears.

The Colonel snatches my piece from me and starts looking it over. *Please, don't look down the barrel!*

"What's your name, Corporal?"

"Morton, Thomas D, Sir."

"How long have you been in the Marine Corps?"

"Almost three years, Sir."

"Going to re-enlist?"

"No, Sir."

Presents my rifle back to me, "I see you have a Bronze Star with Combat V and the Purple Heart."

Release slide, pull trigger. Click. Return to order arms.

"What's the Bronze Star for?"

"For heroic achievement in connection with operations against the enemy in the Republic of Viet Nam…."

"Yes, yes, Corporal. I understand. When do you get out?"

"Next week, Sir."

The Colonel turns to the Lieutenant, who stops shaking his head and glancing to the sky.

"You know you're losing a good Marine here, Lieutenant?"

"Yes, Sir."

"Well, good luck, Corporal."

"Thank you, Sir." *And thank you for not looking down the barrel.*

The Colonel moves to the next guy. The Lieutenant and I are face to face. A disappointed look covers his face.

I remain stoic, in the finest military manner. On the inside I laugh.

They finish inspecting the front side of my rank and come down the back.

The Colonel stops behind me.

"Corporal Morton, when was the last time you got a haircut?"

"Last week, Sir."

"I see." He leans in and whispers in my ear, "I don't think so, but good luck anyway."

He moves on.

I wait in the training office for the IG.

Slagle comes through the door. Comes to attention, bellows "Ten-hut!"

I snap to attention.

The Colonel and Lieutenant enter.

"You're the one getting out next week. Corporal Morton?"

The Lieutenant looks disheartened.

"Yes, Sir."

"Everything in order? Up-to-date?"

"Yes, Sir."

Turns to the Lieutenant, "I'm sure Corporal Morton has everything ship-shape here. Let's move on." Turns back to me, "Again, good luck on the outside, Corporal."

"Thank you, Sir."

He turns, walks past the Lieutenant, "We're losing a good Marine."

"Yes, Sir," glares back at me before following the Colonel out the hatch.

I hope I didn't smile before he left.

1 June

THE LIEUTENANT GETS the last laugh. He makes me come in on the weekend to sign out of the Marine Corps and get my discharge papers.

Last laugh. Yes. But, he has to be here, too.

Gung Ho, Sir!

Pull up to the San Onofre gate, slow down as the sentry comes out of his guard shack. He puts up his hand to stop me. Bends down, looks at me, "You know that expires today?"

He points to the decal on my windshield.

"I know. So does my time in the Marine Corps. So, AMF!"

I floor it and take off. All he sees is the blue smoke from my tires as I haul ass out of there. No speed is near fast enough to put it all behind me. Take one last glance in my rearview mirror. Through the blue haze I laid down from my smoking tires, I see the sentry shake his head as he goes back into his guard shack.

Out the gate onto I-5 South to return to civilian life.

Viet Nam and the Marine Corps.

All behind me.

Whisky Tango Foxtrot Glossary

0100 -- 1:00 A.M.

0400 -- 4:00 A.M.

0430 -- 4:30 A.M.

0500 -- 5:00 A.M.

0600 -- 6:00 A.M.

0630 -- 6:30 A.M.

0658 -- 6:58 A.M.

0700 -- 7:00 A.M.

0715 -- 7:15 A.M.

0830 -- 8:30 A.M.

0916 -- 9:16 A.M.

1035 -- 10:35 A.M.

1145 -- 11:45 A.M.

1410 -- 2:10 P.M.

1535 -- 3:35 P.M.

1600 -- 4:00 P.M.

1653 -- 4:53 P.M.

2245 -- 10:45 P.M.

2300 -- 11:00 P.M.

2330 -- 11:30 P.M.

2531 -- MOS for voice only radioman

2533 -- MOS for radio telegraph operator/voice operator

3rd MARDIV, HQ BN, Comm. Co., Radio Platoon -- 3rd Marine Division, Headquarters Battalion, Communications Company, Radio Platoon

60 -- M60 machine gun

60 mm -- a small mortar

81 -- larger mortar

Acey Deucey -- a form of backgammon

Airedales -- Air Wing Marines

AK47 -- rifle used by Viet Cong and NVA

AMF -- Adios motherfucker

AO -- Area of Operation

Áo Dài -- Vietnamese traditional national attire consisting of a tight-fitting tunic, flowing down to hang as a full-length skirt, open on both sides, worn over loose-fitting pants. Originally worn during the 18th century at the Nguyen Lords court in Hue

Arty -- Artillery

ARVN -- Army of the Republic of Viet Nam

At Ease -- relaxed position with feet apart, hands linked behind back, right foot stationary

AWOL -- absent without leave

Bac Si -- Vietnamese—Doctor

Beat-feet -- hurry

Beaucoup -- many, a lot

Betel nut -- mild stimulant when chewed

Big Green Machine -- Marine Corps

BIT -- Basic Infantry Training

Bitchin -- good, fine, fun

Bloused trousers -- hems of legs turned under and secured by elastic

Boonie cover -- bucket hat

Boots -- besides footwear, recruits beginning military training

Brass – officers

BRASS -- Breathe, Relax, Aim, Slack, Squeeze, for better results firing a weapon

Brevity Code -- code, changed monthly and distributed in pamphlet form

Bronze Stars with Combat V -- fourth highest award for achievement, V for valor in combat

Bru -- see Montagnards

Bulkhead -- wall

Butter Bars -- 2nd Lieutenants and insignias they wear

CAC -- Combined Action Company

C-123 -- twin propeller transport airplane

Cam Lo District -- one of eight districts in Quảng Trị Province, adjacent to DMZ

Camp Carroll -- artillery base south of DMZ and Route 9

Camp Pendleton -- Marine Corps Base, north of San Diego, California

CAP -- Combined Action Platoon, a unit in a CAC

Cattle car -- Cargo trailer with bench seating, pulled by a truck

Chieu Hoi -- Vietnamese—Open Arms. VC, NVA soldiers, and cadres that stop fighting and return to South Vietnamese government authority due to promises of clemency and financial aid. After training, they are assigned to a CAP

Cinderella Liberty -- liberty that ends at midnight

Civvies -- civilian clothes

CO -- commanding officer

Comm bunker -- communications bunker, where all radio traffic is sent and received via various types of hardware

Commrats -- commuted rations, money for not eating in the Mess Hall while living off base

Con Thien -- Marine Corps Combat Base within 3 km of DMZ

Cordite -- smokeless explosive that has a distinct order when activated

Cover -- hat

C-rats -- C-Rations

Crotch -- Disparaging name for the Marine Corps

Deck -- floor, ground

Delta Med -- medical/trauma facility in Dong Ha

Deuce and a half -- 2 1/2 ton, 10 wheel truck

Di -- Vietnamese—go

Di di mau -- Vietnamese—hurry, go quickly

Di di di dit di dit di di dit dah dah dah dah dit -- "Hi son" in Morse code

Di Hao Ky -- Vietnamese—go to America

Dits and dahs -- slang—Morse code

Dóc Kình -- Village where PAPA 5 was located, south of Camp Carroll

Dong Bao -- Vietnamese—villagers, locals

Dong Ha -- Combat Base near the DMZ, northwest of Quảng Tri

Dry firing -- shooting without ammo

E-Club -- Enlisted Men's Club, a bar with food service

Expert -- the highest rate for marksmanship

Field day -- thorough cleaning of the barracks

Field strip the cigarette -- mash up the tobacco and wrapper into small, dust size pieces

Fire Watch -- One-man barracks safety patrol

Flank speed -- top speed

Flying 20 -- $20 disbursed to person going on liberty

FNG -- Fucking New Guy

Freq -- Frequency, channel on a radio

Full Bird Colonel -- Officer whose insignia is a silver eagle

Gook -- derogatory name for Asians

Gunnery Sergeant -- NCO ranked above Staff Sergeant

Halazone tabs -- water purification tablets

Ham and Motherfuckers -- Ham and Lima Beans C-Ration

Hao Ky -- Vietnamese—America, United States

Hatch -- Door

Head -- Toilet, restroom

Hooch -- Living quarters in Viet Nam with a raised wooden floor, screen walls with rain flaps, and tin roof

HQ -- Headquarters

Hue -- Imperial capital of the Nguyễn Dynasty, 1802 - 1945

IG -- Inspector General

Illum -- Illumination

Inspection arms -- Presentation of rifle for inspection

Irish pennants -- loose threads on a uniform

ITR -- Infantry Training Regiment

Jungles -- uniform worn in Viet Nam

Junk on the bunk -- Marine Corps issued gear placed in a precise manner on the bunk for inspection

Khakis -- summer service uniform

Khe Sanh -- combat base in west Viet Nam, near the DMZ

KIA -- killed in action

Kotex -- filter on a cigarette

Liberty -- non work status off duty station

Liberty card -- card carried to show permission to be on liberty

Live firing -- firing fully functional ammunition

M14 -- a rifle

M16 -- rifle used in Viet Nam

M60 -- a machine gun

MACV -- Military Assistance Command Vietnam

Maggie's drawers -- red flag waved in front of target when shot missed

Mama-san -- Japanese—cook, kitchen help, maid

Marksman -- the lowest qualifying rate for shooting

MARS -- Military Auxiliary Radio System used for overseas communication. IE: calls home

MCRD -- Marine Corps Recruit Depot

MEDCAP -- Medical Civic Action Patrol

Medevac -- medical evacuation

Montagnards -- French—mountain people in Central Highlands

MOS -- Military Occupational Specialty

MP -- Military Police

Navy Cross -- second highest award for valor

NCO Club -- Same as E-Club

NCO -- Noncommissioned Officer

NCOIC -- Noncommissioned Officer in Charge

Nón lá -- conical Vietnamese hat, akin to the ancient Chinese peasant hat

NVA -- North Vietnamese Army

O-Club -- Officers Club

OD -- Officer of the Day

Okane -- Japanese—money

On-calls -- prearranged target coordinates for artillery fire

One-holer -- single seat outhouse

Pantaloons -- legs open down the side of each leg and closed tight around ankles

PC -- ¾ ton personnel carrier truck

Peg -- toothpick-like item used in cribbage to keep score. Also, the act of advancing the peg

PFs -- Popular Forces, village militia

Phu Bai -- 3rd Marine Division Headquarters, south of Hue

Pinky -- Nick name for any clerk

Pogue -- REMF and other non-combatants

Pos -- position

Qualifying -- Shooting to earn marksmanship rate

R & R -- Rest and Relaxation, in Bangkok, Hong Kong, Kuala Lampur, Manila, Singapore, Taipei, Tokyo, Hawaii, or Australia

Radio watch -- monitoring radio traffic for a designated time

RC292 -- stationary radio antenna used to increase radio range

Recon -- Reconnaissance

REMF -- Rear Echelon Motherfucker

RF -- Vietnamese Regional Forces

Round eyes -- Non-Asians, usually refers to females

Salty -- experienced and with the language to prove it

Service Khakis -- Summer service uniform

Shaving bowl -- plastic bowl to hold water while shaving

Short -- have little time left in an established time. IE: time remaining in the Marine Corps

Silver Star -- award for gallantry in combat

Six -- CO

Skate -- avoid work

Skipper -- CO

Skunk -- lose by 60 points, an embarrassment in Cribbage

Snapping in -- dry fire aim practice from different positions

S.O.S. -- Shit On a Shingle, a breakfast dish of creamed chipped beef and gravy over toast. Also International distress signal.

Squared away -- perfectly presentable

Steel pot -- M1 steel combat helmet

Tai sao -- Vietnamese—Why?

Tet -- Vietnamese New Year

Three Ss -- shit, shower, and shave

TJ -- Tijuana, Mexico, just across the border from San Diego, CA

Tracer -- ammo that glows red when fired, usually every fifth round

Training NCO -- Non-commissioned Officer of training

Trung Si -- Vietnamese—Sergeant

T-site -- transmitter site

Up and on Shoulders -- An exercise holding an M14 in front of chest, palms forward. Count one, raise the rifle overhead, arms extended. Count two, lower rifle to shoulders, behind head. Count three, return rifle over head as before. Count four, return rifle to front of chest. This is one rep.

Utilities -- work uniform

VC -- Viet Cong

WESTPAC -- Western Pacific, usually Viet Nam

World -- Anywhere but Viet Nam, especially the good ol' USA

Xiangqi -- Vietnamese chess

Zero-dark-thirty -- very early, before first light

ZZZs -- Sleep

About the Author

Whiskey Tango Foxtrot is a compilation of vignettes of Tom's experiences during his U.S. Marine Corps service.

Tom is a retired government employee. His writing skills and editing skills were put to good use in newsletters and various communications and for his community.

Since retiring, Tom has written short vignette memoirs, essays and Letters to the Editor published by the Fresno Bee.

Tom lives in Clovis, California with his wife and three cats.

Made in the USA
Lexington, KY
02 November 2019

56436268R00136